Keep the Line Moving

The Story of the 2015
Kansas City Royals

by

Kent Krause

Keep the Line Moving

Kodar Publishing
ISBN 13: 978-0-692-66370-7
ISBN 10: 0692663703

Front cover photo by Peter G. Aiken–USA TODAY Sports

This is not an official publication of the Kansas City Royals. The book is not endorsed by or affiliated with any Major League Baseball club.

For Jill

Other books by Kent Krause:

The All-American King

Men Among Giants

Behind in the Count

Ninety Feet Away:
The Story of the 2014 Kansas City Royals

Contents

Chapter 1 – "We Still Have a Chance"   1

Chapter 2 – Winter of Discontent   9

Chapter 3 – Reloading   16

Chapter 4 – April: No More Mr. Nice Guy   28

Chapter 5 – May: Quieter Games   43

Chapter 6 – June: Ballot Kings   55

Chapter 7 – July: Gains and Losses   66

Chapter 8 – August: Accelerating   78

Chapter 9 – September: Magic Numbers   91

Chapter 10 – American League Division Series   104

Chapter 11 – American League Championship Series   120

Chapter 12 – The World Series   139

Chapter 13 – Blue November   166

Chapter 14 – Future of the Monarchy   177

Acknowledgments   186

Sources   187

"Get the next guy up. Then he'll get a hit and get the next guy up. That's how we pretty much approach every single game."

Mike Moustakas

Chapter 1

"We Still Have a Chance"

He was arguably the fastest man in baseball. A human rocket who could change a game without even picking up a bat or a glove. Never had he been caught stealing at the major league level. With his blazing 4.29 forty-yard-dash, could he ever be thrown out? Moments earlier, he had stolen second. Easily. And now, with his team down by one with two outs in the seventh inning of an elimination game, he set his sights on third. From there, he could score the tying run to keep the season alive.

Terrance Gore waited as the Houston pitcher went into his stretch. Then he bolted, a blur tearing down the base path. Gore slid into the bag, well ahead of the catcher's throw. The umpire's arms flew out. Safe! The Royals had the tying run just ninety feet away. Or did they?

Houston manager A.J. Hinch challenged the umpire's ruling. After replay officials reviewed the footage, they overruled the call. They determined that Astros third baseman Luis Valbuena kept his glove on Gore as he popped up off the bag for a split-second. Never mind that Valbuena appeared to be touching the runner with his wrist, not his glove. And forget that Valbuena may have nudged Gore off the bag. The runner was out. Kansas City had been retired in the top of the seventh. Trailing Houston two games to one in the 2015 American

League Division Series, the Royals were down to their final six outs in the season. Making matters worse, Kansas City had mustered just one hit since the second inning.

It wasn't supposed to end this way. Falling just one run short in Game 7 of the previous World Series, the Royals had worked all season to take care of unfinished business. Kansas City had cruised into the playoffs with an American League best 95-67 record. With momentum, experience, and determination, this postseason would be different. Surely 2015 would not bring another cruel October defeat for the Boys in Blue.

Despite the dire circumstances, hope remained strong in the Kansas City dugout as Houston prepared to bat in the bottom of the seventh. Fireballing reliever Kelvin Herrera took the hill for the Royals. He had struck out three batters in the sixth. After he again shut down the Astros, KC could work on getting that run back.

Herrera walked Jose Altuve. Not an ideal start to the inning. Kansas City manager Ned Yost summoned Ryan Madson from the bullpen. The new reliever struck out the next batter, before the dangerous Carlos Correa stepped to the plate. On a 2-2 count Madson hung a change-up that Correa blasted into the left field seats. Houston led 5-2. Astros fans heartily cheered this dagger, which all but extinguished any hope for a Kansas City rally. The next batter, Colby Rasmus, had feasted on Royals pitching the entire series. Fittingly enough, the shaggy slugger laced a shot over the right field wall to extend his team's lead to four.

If Kansas City's season wasn't over after Correa's homer, it certainly was now. But Houston was not done rubbing salt in the Royals' wounds. The next batter singled. Then another hit followed. The Astros had runners at second and third with just one out. With the imminent threat of more Houston runs, the Royals' win expectancy plummeted to less than 2%. Yost left his beleaguered pitcher on the mound to take more punishment. Madson somehow recovered to retire Valbuena on a pop out to shallow left. The runner at third could not tag up. Madson then struck out Marwin Gonzalez to end the inning without further damage. But did it matter at this point?

The answer was almost assuredly *no*. Trailing by four with just six outs left, the Royals had no chance. Yes, a year earlier Kansas City had staged an improbable late-inning comeback in the AL Wild Card game against Oakland. But that victory occurred at home, where 40,000 screaming fans could rally their team with chants of "Let's Go Royals!" At Minute Maid Park, the Boys in Blue could draw no such energy from the unfriendly throng that surrounded them. Plus, one team cannot defy such impossible odds twice.

With Kansas City's disappointing exit from the playoffs, sportswriters and fans could start debating what went wrong. Though there are always many factors explaining the outcome of a game and a postseason series, in Royals Nation the brunt of the vitriol would fall on one man's shoulders. With another Royals season ending in cruel defeat, the primary question was: *How did Ned Yost screw this up?*

YOSTED AGAIN

The man had twice turned perennial small-market losers into playoff contenders. He had led a team to the American League pennant. He had nearly won the World Series. One would think these achievements might earn a smattering of respect. One would be wrong. Even as his Royals cruised to the American League Central title in September 2015, Ned Yost remained in the crosshairs. *The New York Times* described him as "the most criticized manager in baseball."

This reputation began nearly a decade earlier when Yost skippered the Milwaukee Brewers. In 2007 his team built an eight-and-a-half-game division lead. Milwaukee seemed a lock to clinch a playoff spot for the first time in 25 years. But a late-season swoon denied the Brewers a postseason berth. Yost's tirades and ejections in the stretch run raised questions about whether he had the right temperament for a big league dugout.

These questions continued the following year when Milwaukee again stumbled late in the season. Ownership grew wary of another eleventh-hour failure. GM Doug Melvin took the near-unprecedented step of firing the manager of a playoff contender with two weeks left in the season. The Brewers made the playoffs, while Yost slinked off the baseball stage in disgrace.

In 2010 Yost returned to the dugout as skipper of the Royals. Despite his reputation, he held the respect of many baseball insiders. Yost's former boss from his coaching days in Atlanta, manager Bobby Cox, appreciated his no-nonsense manner. "You can't beat him as a person or a baseball guy," Cox said. When it came to dealing with the media, however, Yost displayed the charm and tact of a cactus. And so, with the losses piling up during his early years in Kansas City, writers rarely cut the manager any slack. The criticism was even worse in the blogosphere and social media domains.

And so a narrative became established. When Yost's team lost, it was because of his boneheaded managerial decisions. Yost did in fact make his share of unorthodox moves. Allowing a struggling starter to stay in the game. Giving up outs with sacrifice bunts. Not using his closer in a tie game. Relying on gut feelings instead of advanced analytics. Indeed, statistical experts frequently and enthusiastically used their metrics to highlight Yost's lack of managerial acumen.

Even the Royals' winning seasons in 2013 and 2014 did not significantly elevate the level of respect for baseball's top punching bag. Many fans and analysts remained unimpressed as Yost guided his team to the World Series. "There's so much luck involved in short-term success," explained sabermetrics expert Mitchel Lichtman. "Even a .500 team ... can win 90 games and then 12 or 15 in the playoffs on luck." Sorry Ned, your 2014 pennant winners were just lucky.

While Yost's time in Milwaukee and early campaigns in Kansas City did not garner him many accolades, he was learning important lessons during those years. When he first became a skipper, Yost tried to drill into his teams the same focus and discipline he had displayed on the field. Over time, the manager realized that his players had unique strengths to be cultivated. "What I've learned in this job is, players are all individuals," Yost said, "and your job is to let them be them instead of trying to mold them into something that they're not."

Yost's willingness to adapt complimented a confidence he had harbored since his youth. As an undersized high school sophomore in Dublin, California, he once went 0 for 36 at the plate for his JV baseball team. He nonetheless told his school counselors that he would one day play professional baseball. He was right. Yost made it to the major leagues as a backup catcher for parts of six seasons. His clutch home run late in the 1982 campaign helped Milwaukee win the division.

After his playing days, Yost served as bullpen coach and third-base coach for the Braves. His many years in Atlanta allowed him to absorb much wisdom from Hall of Fame manager Bobby Cox. Yost also became hunting buddies with racer Dale Earnhardt at this time. The NASCAR legend once told him, "Never, ever, let anybody who you're around ... allow you to settle for mediocrity." For Earnhardt and later for Yost, there was no difference between second place and last place.

This philosophy would continue to guide Yost after he became a manager. "The difference between 72 and 76 wins doesn't mean a damn thing to me," he once said. During losing seasons he thus allowed slumping hitters and pitchers to face tough late-inning matchups with the game on the line. When his young players failed, a frequent result, fans and reporters would rail against Yost's misguided moves. But the manager viewed the bigger picture. He wanted to put his players in situations that would help them later succeed during contending seasons when the stakes were higher.

Yost furthermore remained loyal to his players. When necessary, he levied admonishments behind closed doors—not in front of the microphones. Ever protective, he showed the same faith in his players that he had in himself as a determined high school sophomore. This might mean keeping a struggling hitter in the lineup even though his average dipped to the Mendoza Line. Or it could mean leaving a pitcher on the mound after issuing a few walks. In 2014 it meant keeping Mike Moustakas in the lineup even when the third baseman could not hit his weight. It worked. "For me, it really helped to get out there, struggle and learn how to work through failure," Moustakas said. "It made all the difference." In the 2014 playoffs the KC third baseman rewarded his manager's faith by hitting five home runs, a Royals postseason record.

After struggling together during three losing campaigns in Kansas City, Yost and his boys learned how to win together. The Royals finished 86-76 in 2013 and then, a year later, clinched the team's first playoff berth in nearly three decades. In 2015 they returned to the postseason. Along the way, the Royals players benefitted from a relaxed clubhouse atmosphere fostered by their skipper. "You pick up clues from the manager," star utility man Ben Zobrist said. "Here, you have the freedom to think that whatever happened yesterday doesn't matter." Centerfielder Lorenzo Cain appreciated that Yost allowed his players to be themselves, both on and off the field. "The chemistry on this team is amazing," Cain said. "That reflects on a manager."

It is a given that baseball skippers face criticism. Fans and pundits have always subjected managers' decisions to intense scrutiny. But in this age of blogs, Twitter, and the instant expressing of mass opinions, the condemnation has hit unprecedented levels. Especially when it comes to Ned Yost. How many managers in baseball history have had their name used as a synonym for an unwise decision? *Yosted!*

But all along, the much-maligned manager maintained that his reputation did not bother him. He avoided reading about himself in the papers and on the Internet. He developed a thick skin. "I don't care too much what people say about me or feel about me," Yost said. "I'm just here trying to do my best for these guys in this locker room."

A VALIANT EFFORT

On that fateful October afternoon in Houston, it appeared that the Royals locker room was going to be a quiet place. A pitcher that Yost had brought in gave up two home runs. The Royals trailed the Astros by four with just six outs left in their season. Hopeless.

Returning to the dugout after the seventh inning, a fired-up Mike Moustakas roared encouragements. With language bluer than the KC batting helmets, the third baseman informed his teammates that they were not going to lose this game. In the midst of this storm of raging determination, other Royals sought to console their beleaguered pitcher. They assured Madson, "It's not going to end like this. Don't worry about it, we got it."

Kansas City's number-nine hitter Alex Rios led off the top of the eighth. One of GM Dayton Moore's big free agent signings the previous off-season, Rios had floundered through a mostly disappointing 2015. He now faced Will Harris, a potent bullpen weapon that had limited opposing batters to a paltry .168 average during the regular season. Whatever dim hopes Kansas City had looked even fainter with this righty-righty matchup to start the inning.

On the other hand, this was the Royals—a team that knew a little something about overcoming late deficits. "We always feel that we're still in games, and we still have a chance," Eric Hosmer said. "That's the mentality for this whole entire team."

Rios drilled Harris's first pitch into left for a hit. Alcides Escobar next stepped into the batter's box. The Royals shortstop fell behind 1-2 in the count. With Harris looking for a strike out, Escobar lunged at a low breaking ball, grounding it up the middle. Kansas City had two men on with none out, but still faced daunting odds. Royals second baseman Ben Zobrist then lined a single into center to load the bases.

Lorenzo Cain batted next, representing the tying run. Maybe this team did still have a chance. Cain ripped a grounder into left. Rios scored and the bases remained loaded. The Royals had closed to within three runs. A.J. Hinch brought in southpaw Tony Sipp and his 1.99 ERA to face Eric Hosmer. Sipp had allowed lefty batters a meager .227 average during the regular season. Even more troubling, the slumping Hosmer had batted an anemic .067 thus far in the ALDS. Kansas City had made some noise, but this matchup did not look promising.

Quickly falling behind 0-2, Hosmer appeared set up for a strike out. But three pitches later, with the count even, the KC first baseman lined a single into right. Escobar crossed the plate, making the score 6-4. And the bases were still loaded. Like a swarm of circling blue sharks, the Royals smelled blood.

Kendrys Morales stepped into the batter's box. The burly DH had driven in 106 runs during the regular season. But he was also a double-play candidate. And that is exactly what Morales delivered with a bouncer back up the middle. Sipp deflected it with his glove, directing the ball right at Houston shortstop Carlos Correa. It arrived with a hop that looked tailor-made for a double play. The twin-killing would score another run for KC, but more significantly it would defuse the rally, leaving the Royals one run behind with just four outs left in the game.

After Correa completed the sure double play, the Royals would remain on the brink of elimination. The shortstop raised his glove, poised to make the play that would move Kansas City one step closer to a season-ending defeat.

Chapter 2

Winter of Discontent

A loss in Houston that Monday afternoon would mark the Royals' second crushing postseason disappointment in less than a year. The previous October, Kansas City had battled the San Francisco Giants to seven games in the 2014 World Series. With two outs in the ninth inning of the deciding contest, Alex Gordon stood on third base representing the tying run. Royals catcher Salvador Perez batted, needing just a single to keep the dream alive. But alas, Perez faced one of the most dominant pitchers in World Series history. Madison Bumgarner had been nearly unhittable in the Fall Classic. The Giants southpaw extinguished the Royals' final hopes by retiring Perez with a pop out.

It was a shattering defeat. Prior to Game 7, Kansas City had seemed like a team of destiny in 2014. Ending a 29-year postseason drought that year, the Royals staged an impossible comeback victory in the Wild Card game against Oakland. They then swept the next two playoff rounds against favored teams. This meteoric rise could only end with a world championship. The Hollywood script demanded it.

But on the final page, the story turned dark. After elevating to heights not seen in more than a generation, Royals Nation came crashing down. Players, coaches, executives, and fans reeled from a devastating gut punch—a cruel ending to what had been a magical ride.

After Game 7 Gene Watson, the team's director of professional scouting, told Dayton Moore that it had been a great season. "What's so great about it," the frustrated general manager snapped. "We had an opportunity to win the World Series and we didn't." Owner David Glass roiled with similar feelings of disappointment. So too did the players. After the final out, Jarrod Dyson lingered in the dugout watching the Giants celebrate. The outfielder could not help thinking it was supposed to be his teammates out there joyously dogpiling. In the clubhouse, Alex Gordon stared silently into his locker. Lorenzo Cain drifted through an interview with glassy eyes. Trying to remain positive, Mike Moustakas urged his teammates to not hang their heads. But that was an impossible request for these men who had given their all. Throughout the locker room, downcast players grieved at what might have been.

The acuteness of the pain made it hard to appreciate the Royals remarkable 2014 success. It all seemed devoid of meaning. Yost described his team's run to the World Series as a long grueling trek, like climbing Mount Everest. But then the loss in Game 7 knocked them all the way down to the bottom. "All that work," Yost said, "really comes down to nothing."

The days and weeks following the World Series brought little comfort. Pitching coach Dave Eiland fell into what he described as "borderline depression." Moustakas felt that the life had been sucked out of him. Dyson lingered in bed for days. Cain watched the postseason games over and over, wondering if he just could have gotten one more hit to change the final outcome. Pitcher Danny Duffy described the post-Series fog as one of the emptiest feelings of his life. Eric Hosmer didn't want to see or hear anything about baseball. "That's just something that you don't really get over," the first baseman said. Yost thought the pain would subside after a week or maybe a month. But the hurt remained. "And finally after two months I figured, OK, it's never going to feel better," the manager said.

Those who rooted for and covered the Royals similarly suffered. Writing for ESPN's Grantland website, Rany Jazayerli opined after the World Series that sports are pain: "What hurts so much isn't that something was taken away from us, but knowing that something amazing and life-altering was very nearly given *to* us." For Jazayerli and Royals Nation, the 2014 postseason had been perfect. "Everything but the ending," he wrote. "And that will live with us for a long time."

Making matters worse was the crushing weight of history that had long pressed down upon Royals fans. Longtime Kansas City faithful knew all about October disappointment. In 1976 and 1977, their team surrendered ninth-inning runs to lose the deciding game of the American League Championship Series to the New York Yankees. In 1980 the Royals lost the World Series after blowing leads in three different games. And then after finally winning a championship in 1985, Kansas City fell into a seemingly endless Dust Bowl.

The defeats piled up year after year. Heading into the 2014 season, Kansas City had not reached the postseason for almost three decades—the longest drought of any franchise in the four major American team sports. During that dreary span, the Royals acquired a national reputation as losers. Jay Leno mocked them in his *Tonight Show* monologues. The commissioner of baseball even considered eliminating Kansas City during league contraction discussions. Ninety and 100-loss seasons became the norm for this once-proud franchise.

A NEW ERA

But the dejection that blanketed Royals Nation after the World Series loss masked a significant development. Barely visible through the clouds of defeat, a brilliant blue light shined. The 2014 Royals marked the dawning of a new era. The team had won more games than it lost. The team had made the playoffs. The team had won the pennant! No amount of World Series heartbreak, heavy though it may be, could change this fact: *the*

11

Kansas City Royals were the American League champions. The dark ages had ended.

The national media heralded this new narrative of Royals baseball. Kansas City's run became the top sports story of October 2014. *The New York Times* ran articles entitled "Now, Royals Can Do No Wrong" and "Royals Envisioned Success, and Then Saw It Through." The *Wall Street Journal* announced that "The Kansas City Royals Want to Rule the World." ESPN acknowledged the validation of Dayton Moore's vision. *Baseball Tonight* held meaningful October discussions about Kansas City for the first time since the show's inception in 1990. ESPN commentator Stephen A. Smith said, "I gotta admit, I love these Royals, man." He and colleague Skip Bayless discussed the team at length on their show *First Take*. Smith described Kansas City's wild card victory over Oakland as "one of the most exciting times I've ever had watching baseball." Bayless agreed, stating, "I'm not sure you can find a better playoff game than that one."

In addition to national sports commentators, fans across the country took notice of the Royals. A poll conducted by ESPN's *SportsNation* found that all 50 states rooted for Kansas City during the World Series. Even California, the home state of the Giants, had more fans hoping KC would win. The Royals, outdrawn by Kansas City's pro soccer team in May, had captured the hearts of the nation by October.

Local fans celebrated with great fervor the new reality of Kansas City baseball. Longtime rooters developed a renewed love for their Boys in Blue. Fan Denise George said the 2014 Royals had brought her family together. "I mean, you couldn't have asked them anything about baseball five months ago," she said. "Now today, everybody's talking about it and it is just great."

In addition to renewing the zeal of longtime fans, Kansas City's October run added legions of new devotees. It became cool to cheer for the Royals. Sports bars in western Missouri swelled with KC fans rooting for their team. AL championship apparel flew off the shelves of clothing stores. Royals caps and jerseys became fashionable again. "You see signs everywhere," Lorenzo Cain said. "You get recognized a lot more and people are wearing our hats and shirts."

The number of Midwestern counties with a majority of Royals fans increased in 2014. Like a conquering army in the board game Risk, Kansas City added new "territories" to its empire. Blue colonies spread northward into Iowa and Nebraska, southward into Arkansas and Oklahoma, and westward across Kansas. And in Missouri, the dividing line between Cardinal territory and Royal territory moved east. New Royals radio affiliates solidified these outposts in the blue empire.

This growing popularity of all things Royal boosted the gate at Kauffman Stadium. In 2014 the team drew 1,956,482 fans, a 12% increase (2,540 per game) over the previous season. This marked the franchise's best season attendance total since 1991, when George Brett still played. The team's television ratings soared as well.

The Royals may not have achieved their final goal in the 2014 season, but things had changed. The team had a whole new identity from just a couple years earlier. A new contender had emerged.

UNFINISHED BUSINESS

Soon after the final out of Game 7, while the Giants celebrated, the crowd at Kauffman Stadium started a chant. "Let's go Royals ... Let's go Royals." Despite the devastating blow of defeat, the spirit of Kansas City's fans remained unbroken. Amid the ashes, a glimmer of hope shined through. There would be another season.

Though it took longer for the players, they too eventually turned their eyes to the future. "It definitely was a few weeks," Cain said, "maybe [a] month into the offseason." But then, mindsets started to change. The thought of baseball, unbearable in the days following the World Series, started to offer some appeal. A distant opportunity beckoned. A new season appeared on the horizon.

One by one the Royals emerged from their malaise. Moustakas turned off the television and arose from his couch. Hosmer resumed his training routine. Gordon added wind sprints to his already rigorous exercise regimen. They and their teammates scattered about the continent found a remedy for their chronic dejection in a new goal: *Win the 2015 World Series.*

The Royals had fallen down the mountain as Yost described it, but they came to view their situation with different eyes than on the night the Giants celebrated. For weeks a debilitating weight, the 2014 World Series became a motivator. The team committed to a quest to win it all in 2015. For some players, it became an obsession. The next season could not start soon enough. Rather than viewing a world championship as a barrier that had proved insurmountable, the Everest standing before the Royals became a challenge to be conquered.

Dayton Moore experienced a similar offseason transformation. Well-acquainted with postseason disappointment from his decade in the Atlanta Braves front office, he moved past the Game 7 loss and started focusing on the future. Specifically, one central question: "What do we need to do to get back?" In the eight years following his hiring as Royals GM in 2006, Moore had helped guide the team from cellar-dwellers to title contenders. Now he would devote himself to making the moves that would vault Kansas City over the top. In this task, he had the full support of David Glass. The team owner felt it was his civic duty to atone for the Royals' World Series defeat. *Atoning for finishing second?* Things had come a long way in Kansas City. Just a few years earlier fans blamed Glass and his frugal ways for allowing his franchise to flounder in mediocrity. Now the owner of the Royals considered anything less than a championship a disappointment.

As the winter weeks passed, the Royals longed to get back on the field. They were eager to build upon what they had accomplished. Moving past the sorrow and misery of the previous season's ending, the Boys in Blue were hungry to take care of unfinished business.

Chapter 3

Reloading

With the 2014 World Series in the rear view mirror, the Kansas City front office began its cold, hard factual analysis of the previous season. Which players should stay? Which players should go? Which players should the team try to add? And how much money is available for the entire roster? These are the questions that every major league baseball team must answer in the offseason.

Kansas City's 2014 payroll was $92 million. Though record-setting in franchise terms, the total ranked only 19th highest among the 30 major league teams. As recently as 2012, David Glass said his payroll could climb no higher than $70 million for him to break even. While that number had obviously changed given the recent bump in team revenues, certain constraints remained. As a small-market franchise with modest television revenue, Kansas City had limits to how much money it could add to its payroll budget for the upcoming season.

Starter James Shields, the Royals staff ace, became a free agent. He had earned $13.5 million in 2014. He would easily command a much higher annual salary in his next multiyear contract—way beyond what KC's budget would allow. Moving on from Kansas City, he signed a four-year deal with San Diego for $75 million. The Royals had an $11.5 million option to retain longtime designated hitter Billy Butler for 2015. But his production had declined in 2014, making that amount less attractive to the front office. Moore still hoped to re-sign the popular Butler for less, but Oakland surprisingly offered him $30 million for three years. And so the long-tenured Royal DH would not be back. Right fielder Nori Aoki also entered free agency, signing with the Giants for more than twice what he earned in Kansas City.

The departure of Shields, Butler and Aoki represented the three largest holes Dayton Moore needed to fill for 2015. Replacing Shields, a workhorse who devoured 450 innings during his two years in Kansas City, was priority number one. To meet this need Moore signed free agent Edinson Volquez to a two-year deal for $20 million. The right-hander went 13-7 with a 3.04 ERA for Pittsburgh the previous year—numbers relatively close to what Shields had posted in 2014.

While Royals writers and fans generally praised Moore's cost-effective signing of Volquez, the replacement for Butler generated far less enthusiasm. To fill its designated hitter hole, Kansas City inked Kendrys Morales to a two-year $17 million deal. The team's new DH had batted just .218 with eight home runs the previous season, split between Minnesota and Seattle. Moore believed the 2014 campaign was an aberration for Morales, who had hit much better in previous years. Royals Nation, for the most part, did not share this confidence in a Morales revival. For some fans, the signing reminded them of KC's questionable moves during the dark ages, like when the team added over-the-hill sluggers Juan Gonzalez and Reggie Sanders a decade earlier. Others asked why Kansas City did not try harder to retain the popular Butler, rather than acquiring a new player who did not appear to be any better.

To play right field, Moore signed 33-year-old Alex Rios to a one-year $11 million deal. The former Ranger had batted .280 in 2014, but with just four home runs and 54 RBIs. As with Morales, Moore hoped Rios would bounce back to higher levels of production from earlier in his career when he regularly hit 15-plus homers and drove in 80-plus runs a year.

Beyond the big three signings, Moore bought a lottery ticket in the form of a two-year $8.5 million deal with Kris Medlen. The right-handed starter had undergone Tommy John surgery in 2014 and would not be available until mid-summer 2015. In the two seasons prior to his procedure, Medlen had posted a 25-13 record with a 2.47 ERA for Atlanta. If he could return to that level, Kansas City would have scored one of MLB's shrewdest off-season deals.

Moore's other signings included the relievers Franklin Morales and Ryan Madson, and a 35-year-old journeyman starter named Chris Young. With the team's five-man rotation already set, the GM hoped these pitchers, along with returning-from-injury Luke Hochevar, would bolster the Royals bullpen depth.

After settling deals with arbitration-eligible players, the Kansas City payroll climbed to a franchise-record $113 million for Opening Day 2015. Just four seasons earlier, Glass had paid his roster a scant $38 million, the lowest team payroll in baseball. A new era had indeed arrived in Kansas City. Unlike in previous decades, Royals' ownership was now willing to pay for talented players who could contend for a championship.

SPRING TRAINING

Chomping at the bit, Mike Moustakas arrived early to the club's spring training facilities in February 2015. Usually one of the first Royals in Surprise, Arizona, this time he found several of his teammates already there. He saw something their eyes. He had it too. Ned Yost noted the difference in his players from previous seasons. "Everybody knows that feeling of winning," the manager said. "Everybody wants to have that feeling again and go one step beyond."

Spring training for the full Royals squad officially opened on February 24, 2015. Finally, work could begin in earnest on finishing the task left unfinished four months earlier. Along with their collective determination, the Royals arrived in Surprise with a new swagger. They were the defending American League champions. Quite a shift from the "maybe this year we'll finally have a winning record" vibe that had permeated Royals spring training for decades. The Boys in Blue now knew what they could accomplish. "A lot of guys turned it up for the [2014] postseason," Eric Hosmer said. "I think we're all feeding off that."

And this year, the Royals had fewer questions to answer than during previous spring trainings. There were no battles for the starting rotation—all five spots were set. The position starters and top three bullpen spots also had no question marks. The roster competition that usually marks a team's spring training was, for the Royals, limited to a few middle relief positions and bench spots.

The biggest question in Arizona involved Kansas City's longest-tenured player. At the end of December, Alex Gordon had surgery to repair a wrist injury that had impaired his production late in the season. He batted just .190 in September and .204 during the postseason. The time needed for post-surgery recovery delayed Gordon's participation in spring training competition. Not cleared to swing a bat, he worked out on his own. He finally played his first Cactus League game on March 21st. Though he went hitless, his return to action indicated he would be healthy enough to start in left field on Opening Day.

Kansas City finished its Cactus League schedule with a 20-10 record, only a half-game behind Oakland for best record. But these games typically carry little weight as predictors of regular season success. A year earlier the Royals finished spring training with a losing record, before going on to win the AL pennant. Nonetheless, Kansas City's stellar record in Arizona reinforced the high expectations among the team's players and coaches.

The Royal bats looked especially potent in the desert. Mike Moustakas made great strides in hitting to the opposite field. His Arizona success fueled optimism that 2015 would yield a substantial improvement on his .212 batting average the previous season. Several other Royals hit well in the Cactus League, including Brazilian rookie speedster Paulo Orlando.

Kansas City's preseason pitching, on the other hand, left something to be desired. The starters especially struggled. Veteran Jason Vargas had the worst time in Arizona, surrendering a herd of gopher balls. New arrival Edinson Volquez also did not dazzle. But spring stats do not count. On Opening Day, these numbers would lose all significance.

Aside from a delayed game due to a huge swarm of honeybees, it had been a relatively drama-free spring training for the Royals. The team escaped major injury, with the exception of losing middle reliever Tim Collins to a season-ending injury. In the battle for the final bench spot, Orlando's hot bat landed him on the 25-man roster.

EXPECTATIONS

While the Royals themselves entered the 2015 season with sky-high confidence, this enthusiasm did not extend outside the organization. Even though Kansas City had reached Game 7 of the World Series a few months earlier, few in the media expected another Blue October. The Royals underdog run had made for a great story the previous autumn, but the traditional diamond powers would restore order to the baseball universe in 2015. Kansas City's pennant was thus nothing more than a fluke.

Before the season, six writers for *Sports Illustrated* issued their picks for the upcoming baseball campaign. None of them predicted Kansas City would make the playoffs. Similarly, none of the dozen baseball prognosticators at Fox Sports deemed the Royals a postseason team. ESPN had a little more love for the Boys in Blue, with four of their 15 baseball experts picking the Royals to make the playoffs. But none of these four believed KC would win the AL pennant, let alone the World Series. Overall, 149 baseball writers from leading online sports publications made predictions for the upcoming season. Only 13 of them picked Kansas City to reach the postseason. And of these 13, ZERO predicted a return trip to the World Series.

Even Internet communities dedicated to the Royals did not see big things ahead. Eight of the writers at Royals Review made picks prior to the season. Seven of the eight predicted 84 or fewer wins. And not one of these writers foresaw a playoff berth for the Royals.

But what about the computers? In recent years statistical analysis and advanced metrics have transformed the process of player evaluation. Using arcane statistical measures that the John McGraws and Connie Macks of yesteryear never dreamed of, sabermetric number crunchers churn out advanced analytical projections for every player in the league. Proponents maintain that these data-fed computers yield the most accurate preseason predictions.

The Baseball Prospectus system PECOTA is perhaps the best known of the statistical prognosticating mechanisms. For the 2015 season, PECOTA in its infinite binary code wisdom projected 72 wins for the Kansas City Royals. Seventy-two? That means 90 losses. Was this some kind of glitch? Perhaps a power surge messed up the data. Or maybe the machine ran the figures from 2005, rather than 2015. Nope, no mistake. PECOTA's cold hard conclusion was that the defending American League champions would finish the season at 72-90.

In case that be deemed an aberration, a second major statistical projection system rendered a similar judgment. FanGraphs predicted the Royals would finish the season with a 79-83 record. Better than PECOTA's gloomy forecast, but still mediocre. Much like the human prognosticators, the computers caught a whiff of Kansas City and plugged their noses.

How about Vegas? Surely winning a pennant would yield some respect from the sportsbooks, right? Nope. Bovada set Kansas City's odds of winning the World Series at 25 to 1. The teams with the best chances of hoisting the trophy at the end of the season were the Washington Nationals (6/1) and Los Angeles Dodgers (8/1). Just a year earlier, when Kansas City had not made the playoffs in more than a generation, Bovada's line for a Royals World Series victory was 33 to 1. Even after a pennant-winning season, not much had changed in terms of national expectations for KC.

Part of this lack of love for the Royals was the stench of failure that still lingered over the franchise. From 1995 to 2012, Kansas City had one, and only one, winning season. Four times in that span the team lost 100 or more games. The Royals may have ridden a lucky streak once, but perennial cellar-dwellers do not make the playoffs in back-to-back years.

Another factor was the lack of respect for Ned Yost, baseball's Rodney Dangerfield. Kansas City may have assembled some talented players, but with their bumbling manager at the helm how far could they go? Many experts believed the 2014 Royals had won in October in spite of Yost, not because of him. His ill-advised decisions would surely derail any chance this team had in 2015.

Statistical analyses revealed more gaping holes in the hull of the Kansas City battleship. The 2014 Royals finished 9th out of 15 American League teams in on-base percentage (OBP) and 11th in slugging percentage. According to sabermetrics, OBP and slugging represent two of the most important offensive categories for determining on-field success. Kansas City, moreover, hit the fewest home runs in the majors and walked fewer times than any other MLB team. The Royals may have overcome these flaws for a brief run in the previous postseason, but the shortcomings would sink the team like a lead weight over the course of 2015. Whatever strengths the team had in defense and pitching would not be enough to overcome such significant offensive gaps.

Wrapping up their Cactus League schedule on April 1st, the Royals departed from Arizona. According to the baseball oracles, both human and machine, the previous season's run might as well have never happened. Kansas City would not return to the postseason.

But the players believed. Their coaches believed. Their fans believed. Royals Nation believed the Boys in Blue were ready to show the world that the previous season was not a fluke.

The best player in Royals franchise history, George Brett spent his entire 21-year career with Kansas City. During that span, he was a 13-time All-Star, three-time batting champion, and the American League MVP in 1980. A driving force in the Royals' 1985 World Series victory, Brett was inducted into the National Baseball Hall of Fame in 1999.
Missouri State Archives

Flags from the first golden age of Royals baseball. From 1976 to 1985, Kansas City appeared in the playoffs seven times, winning two pennants and one world championship. *Missouri State Archives*

Billy Butler (aka Country Breakfast) at the plate at Kauffman Stadium in 2010.

Alex Gordon bats against the Yankees. A starter for Kansas City since 2007, Gordon is the face of the resurgent Royals.

Ned Yost discusses wedding gift ideas with his players during a visit to the mound in 2010. "Candlesticks always make a nice gift."

Spacious Kauffman Stadium has a larger outfield area than any other major league ballpark.

When Royals Stadium opened in 1973, the crown scoreboard was one of the ballpark's most recognizable features. Today, the 84-by-104-foot Crown Vision HD video board remains a leading attraction at The K. *Ron Kalkwarf*

Kauffman Stadium on Opening Day, April 6, 2015
Ron Kalkwarf

Chapter 4

April: No More Mr. Nice Guy

The Kansas City Royals opened their 2015 season at home on Monday, April 6th. The proceedings at Kauffman Stadium began with a special ceremony. Led by GM Dayton Moore, team president Dan Glass, vice president Kevin Uhlich, and owner David Glass, the Royals filed past tables draped in blue to receive their 10-karat gold rings for winning the 2014 pennant. Fans at The K roared as announcer Ryan Lefebvre called each player's name. After the jewelry had been distributed, the 40,000 in attendance directed their attention to the Royals Hall of Fame building beyond the left field seats. There, the American League pennant ascended to join the flags from Kansas City's 1970s and 1980s division and league titles.

The festivities brought warmth to an overcast, drizzly day. This type of season-opening celebration had not occurred for three decades. But as nice as it was to reflect, fans and players alike were more interested in looking ahead. It was time to play ball.

With the departure of James Shields, the honor of starting Opening Day for the Royals went to fireballer Yordano Ventura. The organization remained confident the young hurler could build on his 14-win rookie campaign and emerge as a top-of-the-rotation ace. Opposing him for the Chicago White Sox would be

Jeff Samardzija, an All-Star the previous season with a sub-3.00 ERA.

Kansas City's lineup featured a familiar cast, with the newcomers Kendrys Morales and Alex Rios joining the 2014 veterans. After a scoreless first inning, the Royals grabbed an early lead when Salvador Perez doubled home Morales in the second. Two more Royals scored in the third. Ventura meanwhile cruised along, keeping the White Sox off the board.

In the bottom of the fifth, Mike Moustakas stepped into the batter's box. Ned Yost had seemingly provided more ammunition for his detractors by putting Moose in the number two spot in his lineup. But the third baseman made his skipper look smart by drilling a shot over the wall in left-center to extend KC's lead to 4-0.

Following Moose's homer, Samardzija drilled Lorenzo Cain in the elbow. As Cain stared out at the mound, the White Sox pitcher encouraged him to proceed quickly to first base. The less-than-polite manner of Samardzija's request ignited the Royals dugout. Several players stepped onto the field to express their displeasure with the Chicago hurler.

With a brawl narrowly averted, the game continued. Now even more fired up, Kansas City erupted for five runs in the seventh to put the contest out of reach. New Royal Alex Rios accounted for three of the tallies with a home run to left-center.

The outcome decided, it appeared that the day's drama was over. But in the seventh, Ventura crumpled to the ground after throwing a pitch. When Yost removed him from the game, Royals Nation feared the worst. But the injury turned out to be a thumb cramp that would not cause any missed starts. Kansas City completed the 10-1 drubbing to record its first Opening Day win in seven years.

In the locker room afterwards, Cain reiterated his displeasure at getting plunked by Samardzija. But he took great satisfaction in the victory and the way his teammates had his back. "I know my boys," Cain said. "I know they're ready to go."

The Royals were indeed ready to go. They beat the White Sox two more times to sweep the series. Yost's boys then traveled west to face the Los Angeles Angels, the team with the American League's best record a season earlier. The Royals prevailed in all three contests to complete another sweep.

Sizzling Kansas City moved on to Minneapolis for a three-game set against the Twins. In the first contest at Target Field, Royal bats exploded for 13 hits in a 12-3 pasting. The team upped its mark to 7-0, only two wins shy of the franchise record for consecutive victories to start a season. They had been doing it in familiar ways, with a stellar defense and a dominant bullpen. But the team was also brandishing heavy artillery not seen a year ago. Cain, Perez, and Morales had batted over .400 thus far. Escobar, Moustakas, Hosmer, and Rios were similarly raking. "There's a great mix here of young and veteran players that feed off each other," Morales said. Only a week into the season, many baseball experts started to rethink their preseason projections for Kansas City.

Yordano Ventura owned two wins in as many starts in the young season. In his outing against the Angels, Ventura used his smoking fastball and devastating curve to strike out seven. If the 23-year-old continued this dominance, he would have a shot at becoming Kansas City's first 20-game winner since 1989.

Growing up in the Dominican Republic, Ventura seemed a long shot to make it to the majors. His father had left, and his family could not even afford a bike for him. The determined boy still found a way to get to the baseball field. At age 14, he quit school to work construction—and play ball. But he was scrawny, likely too small to ever catch the eye of a big league scout.

One evening Ventura took the mound at the ballpark in his hometown of Las Terrenas. Royals scout Pedro Silverio watched from the stands. The heat generated by this waif of a seventeen-year-old amazed Silverio. The scout told his boss Victor Baez about the kid's 90-mph fastball. Not long after, Ventura was on a moped riding to the Royals Dominican Academy.

Ventura debuted in the majors five years later. Though still slight by big league standards, the young man had for years developed his natural gifts by heaving concrete blocks, swimming, and playing la plaquita, a cricket-type game. Poised and consistent, Ventura blew away batters with his 100-mph fastballs during a stellar rookie campaign in which he won 14 games with a 3.20 ERA.

But disaster struck in the postseason. Yost called on him to pitch in relief in the Wild Card game. Thrust into this unfamiliar role, Ventura gave up a three-run homer to push his team to the brink of elimination. Though Kansas City came back to win, the young pitcher was crushed. "Please tell them not to lose confidence in me," he texted Rene Francisco, the team's vice president for international operations.

The Royals did not lose confidence in Ventura, giving him the ball in the ALDS and ALCS. Ventura then came through big in the World Series, allowing only two runs in 12 1/3 innings. In the crucial Game 6, he tossed seven shutout innings, putting his team in position to play for the championship the following night.

Despite his success as a rookie and strong start in 2015, Ventura still displayed warning signs. The velocity generated by his small frame created questions about his durability. After a thumb cramp brought an early exit on Opening Day, a calf cramp caused his removal in the sixth inning of his next start. How long could a body that size hold up while throwing that hard?

Ventura's other issue was his emotions. Years earlier, the pitcher's competitive intensity had sometimes led to squabbles with teammates at the Royals Dominican Academy. In his second start of 2015, Ventura glared at Mike Trout after the MVP slugger had lined a hit up the middle. Trout wondered aloud what the pitcher was looking at. After Trout later scored, Ventura got in his face. Both dugouts emptied before umpires separated the two sides.

"He pitches with a lot of emotion," Yost said about Ventura. "He's a real intense competitor." While these qualities fed Ventura's success, the young pitcher needed to learn how to rein in his intensity when necessary.

The Royals fell 3-1 in the second game in Minneapolis, ending their season-opening winning streak at seven. Kansas City starter Edinson Volquez had pitched well, but his offense could not capitalize on scoring opportunities. Not a big deal. Nobody expected the Royals to go 162-0. But the next day, KC pitchers surrendered 14 hits and the team again lost to the Twins. The last undefeated ball club in the majors was now on a losing streak.

More bad news came in Minnesota. In the first game of the series at Target Field, Twins pitcher J.R. Graham hit Alex Rios in the left hand. Yost removed the outfielder from the game, but expressed confidence the injury was not serious. An X-Ray, however, later revealed that Graham's pitch had broken the pinky finger on Rios's left hand. The injury would place him on the shelf for at least a month.

Batting .321 with eight RBIs, **Alex Rios** had been a major contributor to Kansas City's hot start to the season. The outfielder was born in Coffee, Alabama, but lived there only two months before his parents, Israel and Maritza, returned to Puerto Rico. The family settled in the city of Guaynabo, where Alex attended a private school. By his teenage years, Rios grew restless in his middle class life. Though a gifted athlete, he wanted to quit playing baseball and hang out with his friends at the mall. His father had other ideas. "My Dad told me, if I didn't play, I wouldn't be seeing too much of my friends," Rios recalled. "I decided to stick with baseball."

His decision worked out. When he was eighteen, Toronto selected him in the first round of the 1999 draft. As a high school athlete, Rios had displayed skills that Blue Jays scouts believed would make him a five-tool player. That is, a player who could 1) hit, 2) hit for power, 3) run, 4) throw, and 5) field.

After five years in the minors, Rios made his major league debut for Toronto in May 2004. A solid offensive campaign garnered him a fifth-place finish in Rookie of the Year voting. The six-foot-five outfielder made the All-Star team in 2006 and 2007, but his production declined a couple years later. The White Sox claimed him off waivers in August 2009. Rios bounced back in 2010 with 21 homers and 34 stolen bases. He struggled the following season before returning to form in 2012. Chicago traded him to Texas in August 2013.

With Nori Aoki's departure from Kansas City following the 2014 season, Dayton Moore saw Rios as a good fit for right field. Though his production fluctuated from year to year, the outfielder potentially brought power and speed with 165 career home runs and 244 career stolen bases. A sprained ankle and infected thumb limited Rios to just four home runs in 2014, but Royals officials believed he would bounce back. Kansas City signed him to a one-year $11 million deal.

Moore was confident Rios would benefit the Royals on the field and in the clubhouse. "He'll provide us with leadership and experience," the GM said, "and the athleticism really fits our style of play." Rios, for his part, was happy to join a team headed in the right direction. He had played in 1,586 career major league games, but had never reached the postseason. The Royals' World Series run the previous October made KC an attractive destination for the free agent. "Getting to the playoffs is one of the main things for me," Rios said. Once a place that talented players sought to escape, Kansas City now attracted such players because of its postseason potential.

HEEL TURN

After dropping two of three to Minnesota, the Royals returned home for a three-game series against Oakland. Good feelings abounded before the first game when A's designated hitter Billy

Butler received his American League championship ring. His former teammates congratulated Country Breakfast, who had been a mainstay in the Kansas City lineup from 2007 to 2014. Alex Gordon jokingly placed a KC cap on Butler's head.

The pregame festivities also included Gordon, Eric Hosmer, and Salvador Perez receiving their Gold Glove awards from the previous season. Gordon additionally claimed his Platinum Glove as the best defender in the American League.

With three hits apiece from Cain, Hosmer, and Perez, Kansas City took the first game 6-4. But an ugly incident marred the victory. In the seventh inning, Oakland's Brett Lawrie took out Royals shortstop Alcides Escobar with a slide at second base. The Kauffman crowd and the Royals players made known their outrage. Both benches emptied and a brawl nearly ensued as Escobar lay crumpled in the dirt with a sprained knee. Lawrie maintained that he was just trying to break up a double play with no intent to hurt anyone. Ill feelings nonetheless continued to fester. Escobar himself called it a "dirty slide."

The next day, with Escobar sitting out, the Athletics battered Yordano Ventura with five runs in the third inning. Three of the tallies came on a home run from right fielder Josh Reddick. Lawrie batted next. Ventura fired a bullet into the third baseman's left elbow. Once again, both benches poured onto the field. Tempers flared and words were exchanged. The umpire crew somehow prevented a brawl. Interpreting the hit-by-pitch as an intentional retaliation, umpire Jim Joyce ejected Ventura. Oakland went on to even the series with a 5-0 victory.

Kansas City suffered a second setback that day when a strained pectoral muscle sent closer Greg Holland to the disabled list. The bullpen, a foundation of the team's recent success, had lost one of its key components.

The animosity between Oakland and Kansas City continued in the series finale. A's pitcher Scott Kazmir started the fun by beaning Lorenzo Cain in the first inning. After home plate umpire Greg Gibson warned each team, Yost and KC pitching coach Dave Eiland vocalized their displeasure. Gibson ejected them both. Later in the game, Royals reliever Kelvin Herrera fired a 100-mph fastball behind Lawrie's head. Gibson promptly tossed Herrera and then, in the ensuing argument, ejected Escobar and Royals bench coach Don Wakamatsu. While being led off the field, Herrera pointed to his head while glaring at Lawrie. This incensed the A's third baseman, who interpreted the gesture as a declaration to throw at him the next time they faced each other. Herrera said he just meant, "think about it."

Despite the five ejections, Kansas City rallied for three runs in the eighth to win the game 4-2. The Royals took the heated series two games to one. "It was definitely an intense series," Cain said. "A lot of guys got hit by pitches. A lot of bench clearings."

The Royals home stand continued with a series against Minnesota. Again Kansas City took two of three, pushing their season mark to 11-4. They moved into a tie with Detroit for first place in the AL Central.

In the opener against the Twins, Kansas City put the game away with a two-run triple from **Paulo Orlando**, Rios's replacement in right field. It was the fifth triple in just 26 at-bats for the 29-year-old. After a long and winding journey to get to the majors, it looked like the rookie was planning to stay.

Born in Sao Paulo, Brazil, Orlando grew up playing soccer and running track. Baseball was not a major sport in the country and young Paulo knew little about it. When he was eleven, a doctor at the clinic where his mother worked suggested the boy give baseball a try. The physician paid for Orlando's equipment and he joined a club. Though not particularly skilled on the diamond, his speed stood out. Orlando ran so fast he became a sprinter for the Brazilian Junior Olympic team. Being a track star took precedence over baseball, which was something he just did for fun with the kids in his neighborhood. They could only play during the day, however, since the one ballpark in Sao Paulo did not have lights.

Orlando's interest in baseball grew as he got older. In 2005, at the age of 19, he quit track to focus on a diamond career. Orlando Santana, a White Sox scout stationed in Brazil, discovered the speedster. He signed Paulo, who soon gained notice as the fastest runner in the White Sox organization. Though he did not impress at the plate at Low-A or High-A levels, his baserunning made him an interesting prospect.

In 2008 Kansas City traded pitcher Horacio Ramirez for Orlando. His hitting slowly improved as he cut down on his strikeouts. Playing for AA Northwest Arkansas in 2010, he batted over .300. But he suffered an injury at spring training the following season and required surgery. Orlando considered quitting or accepting an offer to play in South Korea. His wife Fabricia convinced him to continue his quest to play in the major leagues.

Kansas City promoted Paulo to its Triple-A team in Omaha, but spending nearly a full decade in the minors—more than a thousand games—tested his resolve. Orlando persevered. In 2013 he played for Brazil's national team in the World Baseball Classic. The following season, he excelled in Omaha. Dayton Moore took notice. "I came away very, very impressed with his at-bats, his athletic ability," the GM said.

In 2015 Orlando batted .319 at spring training to claim the last spot on Kansas City's big league roster. A journey that had taken him from Sao Paolo to the Dominican Republic to North Carolina to Delaware to Venezuela to Arkansas and to Nebraska had finally led to The Show in Kansas City. The 29-year-old became just the third Brazilian to play in the majors. "I'm not that young," Orlando said after making the Royals roster, "but I feel like I'm 17 years old." His first hit in the big leagues was, appropriately enough, a triple.

After winning four of six at Kauffman, the Royals embarked on a six-game road trip. The first stop was Chicago for three games against the White Sox. Kansas City took the opening contest when Hosmer doubled home Jarrod Dyson with the winning run in the thirteenth inning. But once again, extracurricular activities overshadowed the score.

The tensions between the two teams that began on Opening Day intensified when Yordano Ventura hit Jose Abreu in the fourth inning. White Sox starter Chris Sale hit Moustakas the following inning. In the seventh, a quick pitch from Ventura frustrated Chicago outfielder Adam Eaton. The batter took his time settling into the box. After grounding a one-hopper back to Ventura, Eaton shouted something to the mound. The pitcher stepped toward the runner and shouted something back—two words that were rather impolite. After Ventura threw to Hosmer for the out, Eaton headed toward the mound. Umpires restrained the two adversaries, but the benches and bullpens emptied. A full-scale brawl ensued. When umpires and coaches finally restored order, another flurry of punches broke out. This time Cain and Jeff Samardzija were at the center of the fracas. When the dust settled, umpires ejected Ventura, Cain, and Edinson Volquez for the Royals. Samardzija and Chris Sale were tossed for the White Sox.

"It was a messy situation," Ventura said later through his teammate interpreter Jeremy Guthrie. "I got the ground ball and I was unable to control my emotions in that play and it turned out ugly." For the Royals it was yet another unpleasant episode in a season not even three weeks old.

In professional wrestling the combatants are divided into good guys and bad guys. The heroes are called "babyfaces" and the villains are "heels." When a good guy wrestler breaks bad, it is known as a "heel turn." In October 2014, the babyface Royals had captivated the nation with their improbable postseason run. Fans of nearly every team but the Giants rooted for the lovable underdogs from Kansas City. But in the opening month of the 2015 season the Royals had apparently turned heel. Fox Sports called them "baseball's biggest jerks."

What caused this transformation? Wrestler Randy "Macho Man" Savage once turned heel out of jealousy. He accused his tag-team partner Hulk Hogan of lusting after his manager, the lovely Miss Elizabeth. Perhaps similar feelings accounted for Kansas City's heel turn. Were the Royals enraged that other teams were ogling the lovely Ned Yost? Perhaps a more likely explanation for KC's heel turn is related to a change in team identity. No longer the cuddly losers they had been for decades, the Royals entered 2015 as the defending AL champions. Other teams tested their mettle, looking to take them down a notch. Such challenges were met with the blue wrath of a champion. Even their recent adversary Adam Eaton acknowledged Kansas City's new attitude. "They are a young group of guys who go about their business in an exciting and aggressive way," the White Sox outfielder said. "They've earned everything they've gotten and now they want to keep it. You don't expect anything less." Kansas City, moreover, had developed a tight-knit clubhouse. The boys looked out for each other. When other teams barreled into a Royals fielder or beaned a Royals batter, his comrades were quick to respond. A laughingstock for years, the Boys in Blue weren't so funny anymore.

Yordano Ventura had taken the spotlight in April as the most combative Royal. Now bearing the pressure of being the team's top starter, the young man had thus far proved unable to control his emotions. In just four starts he had been twice ejected, and an instigator of rows with Mike Trout, Brett Lawrie, and Adam Eaton. Ventura's competitive spirit had made him a top pitcher in the majors, but his intensity often flared too hot. "He's a competitive guy," Yost said. "He's going to work on controlling his emotions from here out."

NO FLUKE

After their brawl-marred victory over the White Sox, the Bad Boys in Blue held the best record in the American League. On Friday rain suspended the second game in Chicago. After showers washed out Saturday's game, the teams resumed play on Sunday. The White Sox pushed across a run in the ninth inning to win the suspended contest 3-2. In the regularly scheduled game for Sunday, Chicago won again to take the series. Aside from an amazing catch by Alex Gordon tumbling into the stands, neither game included any headline-grabbing events. "I think we got all our emotions out that night and I think it's over and done with," Cain said.

It was not over for the commissioner's office, however. Major League Baseball issued several suspensions for the Thursday night melee in the Windy City. Yordano Ventura received a seven-game vacation; Edinson Volquez would miss five games; Cain and Herrera each received two-game suspensions. For Herrera, the time would be added to the five-game hiatus MLB gave him for throwing behind Brett Lawrie. On the White Sox side, Jeff Samardzija and Chris Sale received five-game suspensions. Fines accompanied these sentences.

The Royals next traveled to Cleveland to open a three-game series against the Indians. Kansas City's bats came alive in Ohio. Feasting on Tribe pitching, Yost's boys pounded out 31 hits to take the first two contests.

Several Royals padded their offensive stats in Cleveland, including **Kendrys Morales** who scored four and belted a three-run homer in the second game. Over the first month of the season, Kansas City's new DH had delivered an impressive .321/.374/.500 slash line (batting average, on-base percentage, slugging average), with a team high 14 RBIs.

Morales grew up in Cuba, living near Havana in a small house with his mother, Noevia. When he was a young boy the Soviet Union fell, creating difficult years for his nation. "Due to the crisis," Morales said, "the school didn't have the best living conditions, the best dining conditions." But one thing that did thrive in Cuba was baseball. And the teenage Morales was among the best young players on the island.

In 2002 Morales batted .324 with 21 homers for his team Industriales de La Habana, completing a standout rookie season in Cuba's top baseball league. The 19-year-old became a huge star in his country. Some even thought he would become the greatest Cuban ballplayer of all time.

The following year, while playing for Cuba's national team at the Americas Olympic qualifier in Panama, suspicions about Morales emerged. Certain officials in the communist nation believed the slugger had been negotiating with a professional baseball agent. His government ordered him home, despite Morales's protestations of innocence. "I never talked to any agent," he said. Government officials did not believe him. Their allegations spawned bitterness in the young man. From that moment on, Morales plotted his departure from Cuba.

The talented ballplayer did not waste any time acting on his plans. He tried to escape to America, but failed. He tried again and ended up in Cuban jail. Undaunted, his efforts to defect continued. Each time he failed, usually finding himself behind bars afterwards. Finally, on his thirteenth attempt, he joined several others from his homeland on a tiny raft floating north. They made it, arriving in Florida in June 2004.

Ready to resume his promising baseball career, Morales applied for residency in the Dominican Republic. This made him eligible to sign with a major league team as a free agent. After Morales played winter ball in a Dominican league, the Los Angeles Angels signed him as an amateur free agent in April 2005. Little more than a year later he debuted in the major leagues.

After a quiet rookie season, the switch-hitting Morales turned in a strong .294/.333/.479 sophomore campaign. Two years later, he contended for MVP honors after batting .306 with 34 home runs and 108 RBIs. The first baseman seemed poised to become one of MLB's top stars until a freak injury derailed his rise. After hitting a game-winning grand slam in May 2010, Morales broke his ankle while jumping on home plate to celebrate with his teammates. The injury would cost him nearly two full seasons.

Morales returned in 2012 with a solid (.273, 22 HRs, 73 RBIs) season for the Angels. Los Angeles traded him to Seattle the following December for future Royal Jason Vargas. Morales gave the Mariners good production the next season before becoming a free agent. After failing for weeks to find an employer, the slugger finally signed with Minnesota in June 2014. Morales struggled with the Twins before they traded him to Seattle the following month. He floundered the rest of season.

Heading into 2015, Kansas City needed a replacement for its longtime designated hitter Billy Butler. So why did Morales, with his anemic 2014 numbers (.218/.274/.338), stand out? Royals scouts considered his previous season an anomaly. They believed that missing spring training and the first two months of the season threw off the designated hitter's conditioning and timing for the whole year. Observing that Morales' strength and bat speed had not declined, Moore and his staff predicted he would return to his pre-2014 production levels. In December, Kansas City signed Morales to a two-year deal worth $17 million. K-Mo's hot start in April 2015 suggested that Moore's DH gamble would pay off.

Kansas City lost the series finale in Cleveland, 7-5. The tribe roughed up Ventura for five runs in 5 1/3 innings to drop the volatile starter's record to 2-2. The following day, April 30th, the Royals returned home to open a four-game series against Detroit. Winners of the AL Central four straight years, the Tigers had owned Kansas City the previous season, winning 13 out of 19 games. If the Royals were to capture their first division crown since 1985, they needed to break the head-to-head dominance of their Motown rivals. Heading into this series, Detroit held a half-game lead over Kansas City in the standings.

Eager to collect Tiger pelts, the Royals unleashed a 14-hit barrage on the visitors. Starter Danny Duffy tossed seven strong innings, and KC prevailed 8-1. Kansas City finished the month in first place with a 15-7 record, marking the second-highest April win total in team history. Their manager was especially impressed with how his squad was clicking on all cylinders. "I'm pleased with the approach at the plate, our defense and our base running," Yost said. "Our bullpen has been absolutely almost unhittable for the most part all month long."

The Royals were off to a promising start in their 2015 quest.

Chapter 5

May: Quieter Games

Kansas City opened May by again defeating Detroit. The Royals were halfway to what would be a huge statement-making sweep over their division rivals. But the next day Tigers ace David Price limited Yost's boys to just five hits in a 2-1 complete game victory. Detroit roughed up KC starter Jeremy Guthrie in the finale to split the series at two games apiece. The loss dropped the Royals a half-game behind the Tigers in the standings.

The home stand continued with a three-game set against Cleveland. Jason Vargas pitched Kansas City to victory in the opener, but the Royals lost the second contest 10-3. In the rubber game, the Boys in Blue pounded reigning AL Cy Young winner Corey Kluber. Back from the disabled list, Greg Holland pitched a scoreless ninth to pick up his fifth save of the year. The series victory over the Indians pushed the Royals to the top of the AL Central again.

And that was not the only good news for Kansas City. In their next game, the Royals would regain the services of Alcides Escobar. A week earlier the shortstop was hit in the face by a pitch, landing him on the seven-day concussion disabled list. Passing the required tests, Escobar gained the doctor's approval to return to the field.

Yet even more good news for the Royals came with the continuing hot streak of **Eric Hosmer**. The first baseman went 5 for 12 against Cleveland, with two home runs and eight RBIs in the three games. His average for the season stood at .324, with a lofty .968 OPS (on-base percentage plus slugging).

Kansas City had selected Hosmer in the first round of the 2008 draft. The highly-touted ballplayer had worked hard since early boyhood to develop his natural gifts. "We didn't have to push or encourage him," his father Mike said. "I'd come home from work [as a firefighter] dead tired, and Eric would say, 'Dad, can we go hit?' He's always had that drive."

Complementing the lad's work in the batting cages and the weight room was a teenage growth spurt that transformed him into a 6-4, 220-pound force of nature. At American Heritage School in Plantation, Florida, he twice earned *Miami Herald* state high school player of the year honors. His mammoth home runs and vacuum cleaner glove drew dozens of pro scouts just to watch him practice. He also attracted the attention of agent-extraordinaire Scott Boras. But retaining the advisory services of the Boras Corporation intensified the pressure on the young athlete. Fans of opposing high school teams chanted "overrated" when Hosmer stepped to the plate. With the support and guidance of his father Mike, his mother Ileana, and his brother Mike Jr., Eric blocked out the distractions and continued to slug monstrous homers with wooden (instead of the more potent aluminum) bats.

David Rawnsley, the national director of scouting for Perfect Game, observed that even in high school Hosmer looked like a big leaguer. "I've seen him hit against the best pitchers in the country," Rawnsley said. "He has a very advanced approach." The Kansas City organization felt the same way, giving Hosmer a team-record $6 million bonus the summer after his graduation. The Royals senior scouting director at the time, Deric Ladnier, praised Homser as one of the finest amateur players he had ever seen. "He is a piece to the puzzle of where we are trying to get," Ladnier said, "and that is to win a world championship."

After two seasons in the minors, Hosmer made his big league debut in May 2011. The 21-year-old first baseman slugged 19 home runs with 78 RBIs to finish third in Rookie of the Year voting. It seemed that Kansas City's next big star had arrived. But Hosmer struggled the next season, slumping to .232/.304/.359. In 2013, after working with hitting coach George Brett, he bounced back, batting .302 with 17 homers and 79 RBIs. His slick fielding skills meanwhile brought home a Gold Glove. While 2014 yielded another Gold Glove, Hosmer regressed at the plate. Missing a month due to injury, he finished with just nine home runs, 58 RBIs, and a disappointing .318 OBP.

The 2014 postseason was a different story. As kids throughout Kansas City emulated his modified Mohawk haircut, Hosmer revived his hitting stroke. In the Wild Card game he delivered three hits, including a crucial twelfth-inning triple, to help fuel his team's epic comeback. For the entire postseason, Hoz batted .351 with two homers and 12 RBIs. His .983 OPS in October suggested he had turned the corner as a big league hitter. When he continued this torrid pace the following spring, Hosmer increased his national standing as one of the game's best first basemen.

After their 4-3 home stand, the Royals traveled to Detroit. The Tigers reclaimed first place with a 6-5 walk-off victory in the opener. Though Kevin Herrera's suspension left Yost's bullpen shorthanded, Kansas City rebounded to take the next two games and the series. KC pitchers limited Detroit to just three total runs in the second and third contests.

The next day the Royals arrived in Texas for four games against the Rangers. After dropping the opener, Kansas City appeared headed for a second-straight defeat the following night when Holland blew a save opportunity. But Alex Gordon hit a go-ahead home run in the tenth and Kansas City prevailed. The teams split the next two games, and the series. The Royals flew home with a one-game lead in the AL Central.

In addition to keeping Kansas City atop the division, the Texas series also marked the return of Kelvin Herrera from his six-game suspension (reduced from seven on appeal). Ventura, Volquez, and Cain had already served their suspensions. The Royals had done the time for their April crimes and May seemed to be a kinder, gentler month. Cain attributed the change to the message getting out that the Boys in Blue would stand up for each other and not let anybody push them around. Yost agreed, pointing out that the way to stop bullies is to punch them in the nose. "That's what happened," the manager said, "and, of course, we're playing quieter games."

PEAKS

On May 15th, Kansas City opened a three-game series at home against the New York Yankees. Back in the 1970s and 1980s, the Bronx Bombers represented the top rival for the George Brett-led Royals. In three straight years (1976-1978), New York bested Kansas City in the American League Championship Series, denying Whitey Herzog's boys a World Series berth. In 1980 the Royals had their revenge, sweeping the Yankees out of the ALCS. Three years later the two teams squared off in the infamous "Pine Tar Game."

The once-heated rivalry cooled in the 1990s and 2000s due mostly to Kansas City's descent into mediocrity. It's hard to maintain a rivalry when one team is contending for championships every year and the other team is languishing in the cellar. But with the Royals' recent revival, "Kansas City vs. New York" regained some of its spark. Especially since the series featured two teams with winning records looking to make the playoffs.

Kansas City bombarded the Yankees with 17 hits to take the opener 12-1. Cain and Morales combined to drive in eight runs, while Moustakas ripped four hits, finishing just a home run shy of a cycle. CC Sabathia cooled off the Royals bats the following evening to even the series. In the rubber game, Kansas City saluted the Negro Leagues by wearing throwback uniforms of the Kansas City Monarchs, while fans at The K "dressed to the nines." Channeling Satchel Paige, starter Edinson Volquez held the Bombers in check to give the Royals the series victory.

If surging Kansas City had an Achilles heel thus far in 2015, it was the rotation. But in their series opening victory over New York, the Royals received a strong performance from starting pitcher **Chris Young**. Signed as an afterthought in spring training, the 6'10" right-hander emerged an unexpected pillar in Dave Eiland's staff.

A two-sport star at Highland Park High School in suburban Dallas, Young attracted many college suitors. He elected to attend Princeton, where he played basketball and baseball. After Young showcased his skills as a freshman, the Ivy League named him rookie of the year in both sports. As a sophomore, the towering Young scored 20 points in a basketball game against a Kansas team that featured three future NBA players.

Young's mound achievements at Princeton mirrored his hoops success. He benefitted from the mentoring of coach Scott Bradley, who learned all about tall hurlers when he was Randy Johnson's catcher in Seattle. Young also appreciated the Ivy League's shorter playing schedule, thereby preventing an overuse of his arm. After Young's second year of college, the Pittsburgh Pirates drafted him in June 2000. Though well on his way to achieving his goal of becoming a professional athlete, Young did not forsake his education. While in the minors he continued his academic work, eventually completing a senior thesis on Jackie Robinson, and a degree in politics.

During his four years in the minors, Young was traded to Montreal and then to Texas. He debuted for the Rangers in August 2004 and turned in a solid 12-7 campaign the following year. After a trade landed him in San Diego, Young seemed on his way to becoming a reliable starter. He finished 11-5 in 2006, and recorded the Padres' only playoff win in the NLDS that year. A hot start in 2007 earned him a spot on the NL All-Star team, but an oblique strain slowed his momentum in the second half.

Recurring arm injuries limited Young to just 36 big league starts over the following three seasons. In 2011 he signed with the Mets, but again struggled to remain healthy. In June 2013 he had thoracic outlet surgery to relieve pinched nerves near his collarbone, a condition that had caused him shoulder pain for years. Despite Young's injury history, Seattle took a chance on the veteran right-hander. Now free from his longtime nerve pain, he bounced back with a superb (12-9, 3.65 ERA) campaign in 2014. After the season, he became a free agent.

Young's revival won him the AL Comeback Player of the Year Award, and drew the attention of the Royals front office. Why was Kansas City interested in an oft-injured 35-year-old soft-tossing journeyman? "At the end of the day, you bet on those players who are great competitors," Dayton Moore said, "great workers and overcomers, and Chris has been able to do that." Moore signed Young to a deal that would pay him a $675,000 base salary, with up to $5.3 million in bonuses based on reaching a set number of innings and games.

When Royals starter Jason Vargas went on the DL with a strained elbow flexor earlier in the month, Yost tabbed Young to fill his spot in the rotation. The tall right-hander's victory over the Yankees was his third straight as a starter, lowering his ERA to 0.94. It appeared that Moore had again struck gold with an off-season signing.

After the Yankees left town, Cincinnati arrived for two games at The K. In the first contest, Yordano Ventura threw seven shutout innings with six strikeouts and no walks. Kelvin Herrera and Wade Davis finished the 3-0 victory. The next night, a strong outing from Jeremy Guthrie helped Kansas City complete the sweep.

Greg Holland was not available for either game against the Reds due to a stiff neck. While the closer said his condition would not be a lingering problem, his earlier stint on the DL raised some concerns. Holland's injuries notwithstanding, the Royals bullpen still owned the best ERA in the majors thus far.

On May 22nd St. Louis arrived in Kansas City for a three-game set. Prior to the first game on Friday evening, the Royals honored Whitey Herzog, the team's manager from 1975 to 1979. After Royals owner Ewing Kauffman fired Herzog, he moved across state to manage the Cardinals from 1980 to 1990. Herzog thus skippered the Redbirds when they lost to Kansas City in the 1985 World Series. With both teams leading their respective divisions 30 years later, Herzog said it would be great to see another I-70 World Series. "Both [teams] are capable of getting there," the former manager said. "I think they both have a great chance."

In the 28 seasons that followed the I-70 Series (1986-2013), St. Louis appeared in the playoffs 12 times, capturing five pennants and two world championships. Kansas City made it to the postseason zero times during that span. This uneven division of fortunes did little to endear the Cardinals to Royals Nation. With the advent of interleague play in 1997, St. Louis stood out as one of the teams Royals fans most wanted to beat each year.

The opening game did not disappoint the home crowd at Kauffman Stadium. Kendrys Morales belted two homers to drive in all five of his team's runs. Chris Young tossed six shutout innings to win his fourth consecutive start and lower his ERA to 0.78. The following evening, Alex Gordon blasted a two-run homer to propel Kansas City to a 3-2 victory in a six-inning rain-shortened contest.

Edinson Volquez pitched all six innings of that second game to boost his season record to 4-3. As the replacement for 2014 staff ace James Shields, Volquez had big shoes to fill. With back-to-back wins over the Yankees and Cardinals, the right-hander was on pace to deliver the production that Dayton Moore had hoped for when he signed the free agent in the off-season.

Growing up in the Dominican Republic, Volquez learned about baseball as a child from his father Daniel. With the continuing support of his parents, Edinson honed his diamond skills as a teenager. When the Texas Rangers signed the 18-year-old in 2001, it was the most exciting moment of his life. "You start playing at nine years old and you never think you're going to be a professional baseball player," Volquez said. "My mom and dad was there [at the contract signing]. They were more excited than even me."

Moving to the United States to play in the Rangers farm system created challenges for the young pitcher. "I was excited to come to the States, but about two months later I just wanted to go back home," Volquez recalled. "I missed everybody back in the Dominican." Trying to learn a new language did not make life any easier. Over time, Volquez learned English by watching cartoons with his minor league roommate John Danks.

Volquez made his major league debut for the Rangers in August 2005. But he struggled in the bigs, losing all four of his decisions that year. He spent most of the next two seasons back in the minors. Texas management, meanwhile, grew disenchanted with what they deemed erratic behavior from their free-spirited pitcher. In December 2007 the Rangers traded Volquez to Cincinnati. The right-hander thrived with his new employers, posting a 17-6 mark and a 3.21 ERA. He earned a spot on the NL All-Star team and finished fourth in Rookie of the Year voting. Injuries plagued him the following season, however. In August 2009 he required Tommy John surgery to repair a torn ulnar collateral ligament and a torn flexor mass. Out for a year, he missed even more time in 2010 after taking a doctor-prescribed medication that yielded a positive test result for performance-enhancing drugs.

Following the 2011 season, the Reds traded Volquez to San Diego. After a decent 11-11 campaign, he struggled in 2012. When his ERA topped 6.00 in August, the Padres cut him. The

Dodgers soon picked him up, but then released him after the season. Pittsburgh took a chance on Volquez for 2014. Once again, a change in scenery worked to his benefit. Studying videos of past games and absorbing the wisdom of Pirates pitching coach Ray Searage helped Volquez correct several mechanical flaws. The right hander bounced back with a 13-7 mark and a career-best 3.04 ERA.

Unable to afford Shields after 2014, Dayton Moore saw an affordable alternative in Volquez. Gambling that the pitcher's resurgence would continue, the GM signed the free agent to a two-year $17 million deal. Volquez arrived in Kansas City determined to succeed. To reinforce the progress he had made in Pittsburgh, he wrote brief reminders to himself, such as "first-pitch strikes" and "three pitches and out." Consulting these notes during games helped Volquez remain focused. Thus far in 2015, he had effectively deployed his arsenal of fastballs, curves, and change-ups to post a sub-3.00 ERA.

The Royals missed the chance for a sweep over their instate rivals when Cardinals hitters tagged Ventura and Luke Hochevar for six runs in the series finale. Prior to this loss, Kansas City had won seven of eight, vaulting Yost's boys to the top of the AL Central by three games over Detroit and Minnesota.

Fan excitement that had been ignited the previous fall remained high through the team's hot spring. The gate reflected this trend. More than 112,000 spectators packed into The K for the three contests against the Cardinals. The Royals thus far were drawing more than 31,000 fans a game. A year earlier Kansas City averaged just over 24,000 a game—11th out of 15 AL teams. As of late May 2015, the Royals were on pace to draw a franchise-record 2.52 million fans for the season.

VALLEYS

On Memorial Day the Royals arrived in New York, ready to show their historic rival that a new sheriff had arrived in the

American League. Unfortunately the Yankees shot the sheriff. And then they killed the deputy. And their horses. Pretty much anything wearing blue that day got filled with lead. Jeremy Guthrie surrendered three first-inning home runs that netted eight tallies for the Bombers. Another three-run blast drove Guthrie from the mound in the second inning with his team trailing 11-0. "He didn't have it," Yost said, in something of an understatement. The final score of the massacre was 14-1.

Jason Vargas returned from the DL to start the second game in the Bronx. Though the southpaw fared better than Guthrie, Kansas City generated only four hits and fell again. Lorenzo Cain provided one of the few highlights for the visitors when he robbed Carlos Beltran of extra bases with a leaping catch at the wall. In the series finale, the Yankees tagged Chris Young with his first loss of the year to complete the sweep.

Following a day off, the Royals flew to Chicago for an interleague series against the Cubs. Kansas City unloaded 11 hits at Wrigley Field to end their four-game losing streak 8-4. Escobar, Gordon, and Perez homered for the visitors.

A fourth participant in the Windy City barrage, **Lorenzo Cain**, drilled three hits in four at-bats to push his average to .304. He also stole his ninth base of the season. With further contributions from his stellar glove work, Cain had edged his way into the conversation for league MVP.

Unlike most major leaguers, Cain did not have an early introduction to baseball. At an age when his future teammates were Little League stars, Cain swatted tennis balls in the backyard. When he failed to make the basketball team as a high school freshman, the lanky teenager looked for something else to join. His mother Patricia had banned him from football, so he asked a friend to help him get a tryout for the baseball team. Though he lacked even a basic knowledge of the game, his natural athleticism earned him a spot on Madison County (Florida) High's shorthanded JV baseball squad.

Working hard after practice to learn hitting and fielding fundamentals, Cain became a decent varsity ballplayer by his senior year. Though still raw, he showed enough potential for Milwaukee to draft him in the 17th round. After five seasons in the minors, the Brewers promoted Cain to the bigs in July 2010. The following December, Milwaukee sent the promising outfielder to Kansas City as part of a deal for Cy Young winner Zack Greinke.

In 2012 the Royals hoped Cain was ready to take the next step to become an everyday outfielder. But injuries sidelined him for more than half the season. Not playing baseball until his teen years had caused the outfielder to adopt poor running habits that stressed his legs. His unorthodox style resulted in several muscle tears. The 26-year-old outfielder needed to learn how to run properly.

After the season, Kansas City trainer Nick Kenney introduced Cain to Oklahoma University's strength and conditioning coach, Tim Overman. Lorenzo moved from Florida to Norman, Oklahoma, to work out five times a week with Overman. The coach observed that Cain would over-stride with his toes reaching forward so his hamstrings had to absorb the force of his foot hitting the ground. After countless hours, Overman taught Cain how to correct his technique so the impact force transferred to his glutes and thighs. In Kansas City, first base coach Rusty Kuntz further helped Cain learn how to maximize his acceleration for stealing bases.

Despite an oblique strain, Cain improved in 2013, playing over 100 big league games for the first time in his career. The following season he emerged as an offensive and defensive force as Kansas City's everyday centerfielder. During the 2014 regular season, he slashed .301/.339/.412, with 28 stolen bases and 24 defensive runs saved (the number of opposing runs a player prevents above what an average fielder would have prevented). In the postseason, he dazzled nationwide audiences with a series of highlight-reel catches in the outfield. His hitting was equally impressive, including a .533 average in the ALCS that helped him earn MVP honors. He batted .308 against the Giants in the World Series. Two months into the 2015 season, Cain continued to deliver with his bat, his glove, and his speed.

Rain washed out the second game between the Royals and Cubs at Wrigley. For Sunday's contest, the teams wore throwback uniforms representing the Kansas City Packers and the Chicago Whales of the 1915 Federal League. Alex Rios returned from the DL to join his Packer teammates. The game settled into a pitchers' duel between Yordano Ventura and Chicago starter Tsuyoshi Wada. With the score tied 1-1 in the eleventh inning, Cubs catcher David Ross singled home the winning run against the KC bullpen.

The defeat at Wrigley marked the fifth loss in six games for the Royals. This late May slide dropped Kansas City a half game behind Minnesota for the division lead. And Detroit lurked only three games back. After a sizzling April, Yost's boys had cooled in May with a 14-12 record for the month. To return to the playoffs, the team would need to right the ship and avoid a prolonged summer slump.

Chapter 6

June: Ballot Kings

When the calendar flipped to June, the Royals' record stood at 29-19. They had played solid ball thus far, but found themselves in second place in the AL Central. In 2014, after a disappointing May, Kansas City went on a ten-game winning streak in June to emerge as playoff contenders. A year later, the Boys in Blue again hoped to pull out of a late spring slide to reassert their claim for a postseason spot.

The team returned home from Chicago for a series against the Indians. Cleveland rode seven strong innings from Carlos Carrasco to take the opener, 2-1. An effective outing from Jason Vargas the next night helped the Royals even the series. But in the finale, every Indians batter in the starting lineup recorded a hit, and the Tribe took the series.

Kansas City looked to rebound against the Rangers. Instead, Texas rookie Chi Chi Gonzalez thwarted the home team with a three-hit shutout. A day later, the Rangers cracked 11 hits to beat Yordano Ventura. Kansas City had dropped nine of its last eleven, the team's worst slump of the year. With a seven-game road trip looming, Yost's boys risked falling out of the race in June as KC had done so many times in previous years. Badly needing a win in the series finale, the Royals allowed Texas to tie the game with three runs in the seventh. With another defeat a very real possibility, a two-out home run in the eighth propelled Kansas City to a 4-3 victory.

The hitter of that tiebreaking homer, **Salvador Perez**, had made clutch late-inning heroics something of a habit. Two decades earlier, when the catcher was a little boy in Venezuela, he hit corn kernels and bottle caps pitched to him by his mother Yilda Diaz. Observing the lad's prowess with a broom, Diaz took her young son to a baseball school. "I didn't take him because I wanted him to be a professional baseball player," Diaz recalled, "all I wanted was for him to keep busy in his spare time and stay away from bad influences." By the time Perez had reached his teen years, his coaches realized that the boy had special talents.

In one of Dayton Moore's first mandates after taking over as GM in 2006, Kansas City increased its efforts to find talent in Latin America. With this new emphasis, the team added a dozen scouts to focus on international prospects. That summer, Royals scout Orlando Estevez observed the amazing coordination displayed by a towering catcher with a bright smile in Valencia, Venezuela. Though some questions remained about whether the cheerful 16-year-old could hit, Kansas City signed Perez for $65,000. The young catcher used this money to buy a house he would share with his grandmother and mother, who had diligently supported his baseball aspirations.

It did not take long for Perez to wow the coaches in the Royals organization with his deft footwork, soft hands, and bazooka arm. At an A-level game at spring training one year, Ned Yost clocked Perez throwing out a baserunner with an astounding mitt to glove time of 1.83 seconds (1.9 seconds is the benchmark for excellence). The catcher also impressed Yost with how quickly he learned the other aspects of his position, including game-calling. "He picks things up really quick," the manager said, "… learning the pitchers, what they like to do, learning the opposition, he's done a nice job." When on an injury rehabilitation assignment in 2010 for the Royals Class A

Wilmington (Delaware) team, Alex Gordon observed the defensive skills of the 6-3, 240-pound catching prospect. "I kind of knew, when I was watching him, that this guy was going to be pretty special," Gordon said. "And being the size that he was, moving how he did, it was something you could definitely spot."

Kansas City promoted Perez to the majors in August 2011. Though a knee injury the following spring training sidelined him until July, he hit an impressive .301 with 11 home runs in the second half of 2012. His productive bat continued with a .292/.323/.433 slash line in 2013. Perez contributed even greater value with his ability to block pitches, throw out base stealers, and call games. The catcher furthermore studied video of opposing batters to enhance his effectiveness at selecting pitches. "He's very good at knowing how each pitcher's strength matches up to each hitter," Dave Eiland said. By the end of the 2014 season, Perez's skills had earned him back-to-back All-Star selections and back-to-back Gold Gloves.

Perez's contributions extended off the field as well. An avid dancer with a high-wattage grin, the big catcher with the booming voice brought a lively presence to the clubhouse. Following Alcides Escobar's example, he sprayed on Victoria's Secret perfume before games. Following victories, he snuck up behind teammates during interviews with Joel Goldberg to douse them with a bucket of Gatorade or ice water. These "Salvy baths" became a Royals tradition in 2015. Wielding his ever-present iPhone, he relentlessly stalked teammates to capture candid footage for humorous Instagram posts. Though a favorite target of Salvy's antics, Lorenzo Cain appreciated what his friend meant to the team. "He fights on the field, but in the clubhouse he keeps it relaxed and laid back," Cain said. "No matter what happens, he doesn't change."

An iron horse for the Royals in their drive to the 2014 postseason, Perez drove in the game-winning run in the historic Wild Card game against Oakland. Despite being worn down by catching 157 games, the bruised backstop batted .333 in the World Series against the Giants. But popping out in the ninth inning of Game 7 ended the season on a sour note. Like his teammates, Salvy hoped to erase that memory with a different ending in 2015.

SURGE

Perez's game-winning home run against Texas reinvigorated the Royals for their upcoming seven-game road trip. Kansas City won the series opener in Minnesota behind six shutout innings from starter Jason Vargas. The southpaw picked up his fifth win of the year, but a few days later landed on the disabled list due to a strained flexor muscle in his elbow. With Danny Duffy on the sidelines with left biceps tendinitis, Yost's starting rotation had no active southpaws.

The following night Chris Young delivered another dominant start and Kansas City rolled 2-0. In the series finale at Target Field, Alex Gordon drilled a three-run homer and Edinson Volquez tossed seven strong innings to complete the KC sweep. After getting ejected for arguing a third-strike call, Minnesota outfielder Torii Hunter provided added entertainment for the fans by stripping off his jersey in an impromptu burlesque show. Riding a four-game winning streak, the Boys in Blue again climbed to the top in the AL Central.

The Royals next traveled to St. Louis, where Redbird starter Jaime Garcia silenced their bats with eight shutout innings. In addition to taking the loss, Yordano Ventura had to be removed after three innings due to numbness in his throwing hand. A fluid buildup had placed pressure on his ulnar nerve, causing Ventura to lose sensation in his thumb and two fingers. Team trainers nonetheless hoped the right-hander would not miss a start. Gordon and Perez homered the next day, but Kansas City got little else and fell again at Busch Stadium.

The Royals next headed to Milwaukee for two games at Miller Park. Kansas City's bats came alive in Wisconsin, blasting out 30 hits to pick up two victories. In the second game, Chris Young became the first Royals pitcher since 1972 to collect three RBIs in a game. The Royals and Brewers traveled to Kauffman for two more games. Different venue, but the same result. Kansas City won both contests, completing four straight wins against The Crew. The second victory at The K marked the 411th win for Ned Yost as Royals skipper. This moved him past Whitey Herzog as the winningest manager in team history. Yost said he did not feel like he was in the same class as Herzog and Dick Howser. "This is an organizational-wide achievement and I'm proud to be part of that," Yost said after the historic win.

Royal bats had exploded for 55 hits in the four games against Milwaukee. Leadoff hitter **Alcides Escobar** helped ignite this barrage, batting 8 for 18 with six RBIs against his former team. The shortstop's contributions with his bat and his glove were a big reason his team remained atop the standings.

Escobar started learning the game of baseball as a three-year-old in Venezuela. Growing up, the boy idolized fellow Venezuelan Omar Vizquel—winner of nine Gold Gloves at shortstop. "I was always looking up to him [Vizquel] with everything that I do," Escobar said. "And Derek Jeter, too." Young Alcides worked hard to match the defensive skills of his heroes. Catching the eye of Milwaukee scouts, he signed with the Brewers for $35,000 in 2003 when he was 16 years old.

Rising through the Brewers farm system, Escobar became Milwaukee's everyday shortstop in 2010. He dazzled with his glove, but struggled offensively. In the offseason, Brewers general manager Doug Melvin looked to add a top-of-the-rotation starter to contend for the NL pennant. Kansas City's Zack Greinke, winner of the 2009 Cy Young, topped his wish list. Greinke had made it no secret that he wanted to be liberated from the Royals and their losing ways. Dayton Moore, looking to build up a strong defensive corps, coveted the young gloves Milwaukee had at shortstop and centerfield. In December 2010, Melvin sent Escobar and Cain (and pitching prospects Jake Odorizzi and Jeremy Jeffress) to Kansas City for Greinke and shortstop Yuniesky Betancourt.

Though acquired for his defense, Escobar demonstrated sparks of offensive potential his first season with the Royals. Kansas City wasted little time signing their new shortstop to a four-year deal for $10.5 million with club options that could push the amount to $21.75 million for six years. "He's a Gold Glove-caliber shortstop," Yost said after the signing. "I personally think he's the best shortstop in the American League, if not in all of baseball." Moore echoed these sentiments. "You can't win championships without a shortstop," the GM said, "and he [Escobar] gives you the ability to stabilize your infield."

The following season, Escobar improved his offense by batting .293 with 35 stolen bases. But he regressed in 2013, hitting just .234 with a woeful .259 OBP. Yost absorbed much criticism for not pinch hitting for the flailing shortstop in key situations. But the manager wanted him to learn. Escobar failed more often than not that season, but he gained experience that would pay off in later years when the Royals were contenders. Escobar bounced back in 2014 with a .285/.317/.377 offensive campaign, while his amazing range and laser arm elevated Kansas City's defense. He batted over .300 in the World Series against the Giants.

A series of dazzling plays the first half of 2015 left many experts talking Gold Glove for Escobar—nicknamed "El Mago" (the magician) for his defensive tricks. He also contributed to the positive energy to the clubhouse. "He does it all," Cain said about the shortstop. "He hits leadoff, plays hard, steals bags, takes bases and is a great teammate." Salvador Perez concurred. "He has great energy and effort," the catcher said about Escobar. "He always plays hard and tries to help us win the game."

Winners of eight of their last 10, the Royals had extended their division lead to three-and-a-half games. The team next welcomed Boston to The K. In the series opener, the Red Sox shelled Yohan Pino, a recent KC call-up from Triple-A Omaha. The right-hander was filling in for Ventura, who had been placed on the DL due to an ulnar nerve inflammation. The following night, Perez and Kendrys Morales homered to help the Royals take the second game. But Boston battered Chris Young in the finale, thrashing the home team 13-2.

#VOTEOMAR

The Royals flew west to start a nine-game road trip in Seattle. The opener at Safeco Field looked to be a sure loss since Kansas City, with three starting pitchers on the DL, had to send journeyman Joe Blanton to the mound to face Felix Hernandez, a former Cy Young winner and one of the best pitchers in the league. But Blanton, who had retired from baseball a year earlier following a disastrous 2-14 campaign for the Angels, allowed only two hits and one run over six innings to dethrone King Felix. Former Royals prospect Mike Montgomery shut out KC the next night. With Danny Duffy back from the DL to start the third contest at Safeco Field, Kansas City's offense flexed its muscles in an 8-2 victory to take the series.

In the series finale in Seattle, the Royals received a big spark from **Omar Infante**. The second baseman went three for four, providing a key blow with a bases-clearing double in the fourth. Kansas City coaches hoped this outburst represented a sign of things to come from their veteran infielder.

Like his teammates Perez and Escobar, Infante caught the eye of big league scouts as a teenager in Venezuela. Detroit signed the 17-year-old in April 1999. The young ballplayer faced adversity in his early career, losing his brother and father over the next two years. Honoring their memory, Infante worked hard to rise through the minor league ranks. By 2002 several observers considered him the top prospect in the Tigers farm system. Detroit coach Doug Mansolino raved about Infante's potential. "He's got great actions and instincts," the coach said, "everything you look for in an infielder."

Infante emerged as Detroit's everyday second baseman in 2004. He complimented his steady glove work with surprising power for a middle infielder. When Infante struggled at the plate the following season, the Tigers limited his playing time. After the 2007 campaign, Detroit traded him to the Cubs, who immediately shipped him to the Braves. The move to Georgia revived Infante's career. He delivered three solid seasons, earning an All-Star selection in 2010 when he batted .321/.359/.416. Atlanta dealt the second baseman to Florida the following off-season, and Detroit reacquired him midway through the 2012 season.

After a strong 2013 campaign (.318, 10 HRs, 51 RBI) for the Tigers, Infante became a sought-after free agent. Dayton Moore believed the infielder could bolster his team's defense and provide stability at second base. The Royals had struggled for years to find the answer at that position. Also hopeful that a seasoned veteran like Infante would elevate Escobar's play at shortstop, Kansas City signed the second baseman to a four-year $30.25 million deal.

Infante's first season in a Royals uniform did not go quite like he or Moore envisioned. An early-season fastball lacerated and bruised his jaw. An ailing back sent him to the disabled list in May. A sore elbow bothered him most of the spring, and an aching shoulder plagued him all season. Infante battled through the pain and contributed to his team's march to the postseason by playing 135 games and driving home a career-high 66 runs. Moore recognized these contributions. "It seems like to me, he's always gotten on base at the right time or gotten the big hit," the GM said. "He's been in the middle of a lot of our success." Eric Hosmer also noted the key role Infante played. "Just the way he carries himself, how he has an effect on Esky, and how he has an effect on all the guys in here," Hoz said. "He's a leader, man."

By the 2014 playoffs, Infante's persisting shoulder ailment convinced him to take the powerful drug Toradol to manage the pain. The stronger pills seemed to help. Infante batted .308 in the ALCS and .318 with a homer and five RBIs in the World Series. These numbers suggested that the second baseman would bounce back from his disappointing (.632 OPS) regular season.

But he struggled again in 2015, batting just .234 over the first three months. Speculation increased that Yost might be looking to make a change at second base.

After taking two of three from Seattle, the Royals traveled south for a three-game set against Oakland. Given that these two teams had nearly traded blows in each of the three games they played in April, many fans expected tensions to boil over again. Yost downplayed the drama. "Nobody on my team has even mentioned it or thought about it," the manager said, "and I doubt very seriously anybody over there has."

That assessment proved to be correct. Royals reliever Franklin Morales hit Oakland catcher Stephen Vogt with a pitch in the first game. But Vogt quickly defused the situation by declaring it unintentional. Aside from the spirited booing of Kelvin Herrera by Athletics fans, the contest featured no signs of the previous bad blood. The second and third games at O.co Coliseum similarly passed without incident. Of greater significance were the scores. Riding strong outings from its starting pitchers—Volquez, Young, and Guthrie—Kansas City swept all three games from the Athletics to improve to 44-28.

By this point in the season, the Royals were making headlines for something other than brawling. In 2015 Major League Baseball revised its decades-long process for selecting All-Star Game starters. Instead of using paper ballots distributed at ballparks, the voting would be done online. Fans could fill out 35 Internet ballots per email address each day. When MLB started releasing the current vote totals in June, some surprising results came in for the American League. Members of the Royals led at eight of the nine lineup positions (managers and players selected the pitchers). Reigning MVP Mike Trout was the only non-Royal who would have started for the AL All-Star team if no changes occurred among the vote leaders.

Several Royals, such as Alex Gordon, Salvador Perez, Lorenzo Cain, and Alcides Escobar were legitimate candidates as All-Star starters. But Eric Hosmer, though enjoying a fine season, led at first base over Miguel Cabrera, who topped the AL in slugging and OBP. Similarly, Mike Moustakas held a lead in balloting over third baseman Josh Donaldson, despite the latter's 50-point advantage in OPS.

The most eyebrow-raising result was second baseman Omar Infante's ballot lead over Houston's Jose Altuve. Infante, one of the worst hitters in the league, was batting 60 points lower than Altuve, the reigning AL batting champion. Outrage and accusations of fraud followed. Tigers pitcher David Price called the process a joke. ESPN baseball analyst Jim Bowden said the All-Star voting system was broken. Critics accused Royals fans of setting up email accounts just to cast votes for their players— a modern-day cyber version of stuffing the ballot box.

Major League Baseball assured skeptics that the voting results were legitimate and that no conspiracy existed. MLB president of business and media Bob Bowman explained that the Royals' passionate fan base and growing team popularity were the reasons for the results. "You are dealing with a great outpouring of support for this team, and you see it at the park, with [Internet] traffic, and they're now in the top 10 in merchandise sales," Bowman said.

Kansas City radio talk show host Nate Bukaty offered a similar assessment, pointing out that the online vote encouraged younger fans to get involved. "And if there's one city where young fans are really excited about their team," Bukaty said, "it's Kansas City." Royals vice president of marketing and business development Mike Bucek concurred. "People in this area are highly motivated," Bucek said. "These players have bonded with this fan base, and the fans want to see them play in Cincinnati [site of the All-Star Game]."

Despite these explanations, fans in other American League cities remained rankled. This brought much delight to Royals Nation. Supporters of the Boys in Blue continued voting 35 times a day per email address for their heroes. They used social media sites, such as Twitter, to spread the word. The #VoteRoyals hashtag went viral. Legions of Royals faithful campaigned to get Infante into the starting All-Star lineup. #VoteOmar became a trending topic on Twitter. Not because KC fans thought he deserved it, but to show their pride for a team that had been maligned for decades by the rest of the league. Nearly every year during the dark ages, only one Royal represented the team at the All-Star Game. Each vote from Kansas City fans in 2015 further distanced the current squad from the Mark Redman era.

Infante himself admitted his production was not All-Star worthy. "But I don't have control over that," the second baseman said. "The fans voted for me. I appreciate that." Yost also expressed his appreciation to his team's fans for voting. And to those whining about the process, Yost offered some obvious advice: "Everybody's free to vote," the manager said. "It's not like, 'Oh, nobody else can vote but the Royals fans.'"

After sweeping the Athletics, Kansas City concluded its road trip in Houston. In a battle of teams with the two best records in the American League, the Astros scored early and often to take the opener 6-1. The next night the Royals fell to Houston ace Dallas Keuchel. In the finale, played on July 1st, Kansas City's offense woke up, but not enough. Astros hitters banged out 10 hits in a 6-5 victory to complete the sweep.

The Royals had built an impressive 44-31 record over the first three months of the season. They held a four-and-a-half game lead in the division. Despite getting swept by a potential playoff opponent, Kansas City's prospects remained bright as the season approached the halfway point.

Chapter 7

July: Gains and Losses

Departing Houston, the Royals returned to Kansas City for an 11-game home stand. In the first of four contests against Minnesota, Twins starter Kyle Gibson extended their losing streak to four. Now trailing the Royals by only 3.5 games, Minnesota fostered hopes of sweeping the series to pull within a half-game of the division lead. Lorenzo Cain made sure that did not happen when he slid home with the winning run in the tenth inning of the second contest. The Twins captured the next game, on the Fourth of July, before Cain scored another game-winning run in the finale to give Kansas City a series split with its closest pursuer.

During the Minnesota series, fans dropped off thousands of boxes of colorful bandages at The K. A few days earlier, seven-year-old Royals fan Noah Wilson had succumbed to leukemia. Befriended by Eric Hosmer during his medical battles, Noah had started a campaign to collect colorful Band-Aids for children similarly fighting cancer. Upon learning of his passing, the Royals honored his legacy by helping collect donations for Noah's Bandage Project.

After the Twins left town, Kansas City played a doubleheader against Tampa Bay. Paulo Orlando slugged a tie-breaking grand slam in the bottom of the ninth to take the opener. In the nightcap, Alcides Escobar delivered a bases-clearing double to help KC win again. The doubleheader sweep featured a monster day from Alex Gordon. The left fielder cracked seven hits in the two games, including a home run, a double, and six RBIs.

Kansas City continued its barrage with 26 more hits over the next two days against the hapless Rays pitchers. The Royals swept the four-game series, but faced a major setback. When chasing a long fly ball from Rays hitter Logan Forsythe, Gordon stumbled awkwardly and heard something pop. He lay face down in the warning track dirt as trainers raced across the field. Fans at The K held their breath, fearing a season-ending injury. While that worst-case scenario did not happen, the severe groin strain that Gordon suffered would deprive Kansas City of its star outfielder for at least two months.

Alex Gordon was born in Lincoln, Nebraska, the year before the Royals won their first World Series. While Kansas City dropped from top contender to perennial loser in the 1990s, Gordon emerged as a star for the Lincoln Rebels select team. He continued to impress in high school, slugging jaw-dropping home runs that soared far beyond outfield fences. Other teams grew so fearful of Gordon, they intentionally walked him—even when his coach batted him leadoff.

Remaining in Lincoln, Gordon played college ball for the University of Nebraska. Even as a collegiate athlete, he pursued a healthy diet, rigorous training regimen, and blue-collar work ethic. Continuing to destroy opposing pitching, the star third baseman led the Cornhuskers to the College World Series. Following Gordon's third dominant season with Nebraska, Kansas City selected the junior with its first pick in the 2005 draft. Royals fans rejoiced at this selection of a "hometown" Midwestern boy—Lincoln is only 200 miles from Kansas City. With his sandy-blond hair and sweet left-handed swing, the third baseman was hailed as the next George Brett. Such comparisons to a Hall of Famer, however, did not prove helpful to the young player's development.

Gordon struggled through a subpar (.247/.314/.411) rookie season in 2007. Though his numbers improved the next year, a torn hip shelved him through much of the 2009 campaign. After he broke his thumb the following spring, Gordon's struggles worsened in 2010. His batting average dipped below .200 and his fielding at third base was among the worst in the league. In May, Dayton Moore told Gordon the team was sending him to AAA Omaha. The GM added that his days at third base were over—the team wanted him to give left field a try. "It was not a good moment in my career, to be honest with you," Gordon said. Baseball analysts viewed the demotion and position change in darker terms. "More evidence they've given up on him," tweeted ESPN's Rob Neyer, expressing a common opinion.

The Royals assigned field instructor Rusty Kuntz the task of teaching Gordon how to play left field. His student proved eager and ready to work. When Kuntz arrived at the ballpark, he found his charge already there waiting for him. Gordon put in long hours learning and applying Kuntz's 75 outfielding rules. He logged double sessions "power shagging" (fielding batting practice balls like hits in a real game). The team filmed his intense outfield workouts to instruct minor leaguers. "It's about repetition," Gordon said, "going out and playing every day."

The hard work paid off. In 2011, Gordon's first full season in left field, he led the majors with 20 assists. His rifle arm and keen fly ball-tracking skills earned him a Gold Glove at season's end. It would be the first of four consecutive Gold Gloves for the best fielding outfielder in the game. "He's like a human dart," said Royals TV commentator Rex Hudler. "He would stick to the ball all the way to the wall." From 2011 to 2014, Gordon led all left fielders with 62 assists, 87 DRS (defensive runs saved) and a dWAR (defensive wins above replacement) of 7.0. In 2014 Gordon won the Platinum Glove as the American League's best overall defender.

Gordon also produced at the plate. He batted over .300 in 2011, led the majors in doubles in 2012, and drove in 70-plus runs four straight seasons. Though hampered by a wrist injury in

2014, he led his team with 19 homers and 74 RBIs. He drove in 11 more runs during the Kansas City's postseason run. And in Game 7 of the World Series, with his team down to its final out, he delivered a key hit that put the tying run ninety feet away.

If the Royals hoped to return to the World Series in 2015, they needed Gordon to remain productive. Mike Moustakas called him the team's captain. "He's what gets us going and what keeps us going," Moose said. Recovering from off-season wrist surgery, Gordon was slashing a robust .279/.394/.457 when he went down. But now his team would have to carry on without him for two months. And since Gordon was likely a free agent at the end of the year, Royals fans wondered how many more times they would see Number 4 in left field.

Following their sweep of the Rays, Kansas City hosted Toronto for a three-game set—the last series before the All-Star break. Danny Duffy and the H-D-H (Herrera-Davis-Holland) bullpen trio shut out the Blue Jays in the opener. The next day, Toronto starter Mark Buehrle and two relievers limited Kansas City to just five hits to even the series. In the finale, the Royals committed an uncharacteristic four errors while blowing a seven-run lead to fall behind 8-7. But Paulo Orlando came to the rescue with a tie-breaking homer in the eighth, and Kansas City won a wild rubber game 11-10.

The victory improved the Royals' record to 52-34. For the first time since 2003, Kansas City headed into the break with a division lead.

THE ALL-STAR GAME

In the not-so-distant past, the All-Star break held little meaning for the Royals. The team was usually out of contention by July, and often did not have any stellar players on its roster. But league rules mandated that an All-Star squad include at least one player from each team in the league. In the 1990s and 2000s, the Royals rarely exceeded this one-player All-Star minimum. And some of these players were "stars" only in the loosest definition of the term.

Things had changed by 2015. With a tidal wave of online votes, by late June it appeared that eight of the nine AL position starters would be Royals. This news sparked a national media campaign that spurred voting in other cities. Major League Baseball, meanwhile, citing a concern about "improper voting," threw out 60 million votes. Apparently "The Man" could not tolerate the idea of Omar Infante starting in the All-Star Game.

When the dust settled and MLB tallied the final results, four Royals topped the fan vote at their positions: Alex Gordon (OF), Lorenzo Cain (OF), Alcides Escobar (SS), and Salvador Perez (C). In addition, Mike Moustakas (3B) won the "Final Vote" balloting for the last spot on the AL roster. As skipper of the previous year's pennant winners, Ned Yost managed the American League All-Stars. He selected Kelvin Herrera and Wade Davis as pitchers for the AL squad.

Kansas City had a franchise record seven All-Star players. That is only three fewer than the team had in the entire decade of the 1990s. Gordon explained the ASG voting phenomenon by pointing to the Royals' huge fan support. "Winning brings attention, and that's what we've been doing," the left fielder said. "I think we play with a lot of energy, a lot of fun. People have noticed it." SungWoo Lee, the Royals superfan who gained fame the previous August when he traveled from South Korea to watch his favorite team at The K, agreed. "The Royals got lots of love and attention from all over the states as the feel-good underdog story last year," Lee said, "then another strong season record, and energetic, play-hard Royals keep drawing attention from baseball fans."

For Gordon and Perez, 2015 marked their third straight All-Star selections. But for the second consecutive year, an injury would prevent Gordon from playing in the game. "In back-to-back years, it's frustrating," the left fielder said. "It's not what we play for, but it's definitely an honor to be in the All-Star Game." For the other five Royals, it marked their first ever

Midsummer Classic. Escobar was especially moved when he received the news. "I felt like crying," the shortstop said. "Everything was just coming over me. It's a dream come true."

Mike Moustakas found even greater meaning in his selection as an All-Star. His mother Connie was in the hospital at the time battling cancer. "I wanted to make her proud every single day," Moustakas said. "And to be named to my first All-Star team when all that was going on was pretty special."

Kansas City selected Moustakas in the first round of the 2007 draft. He was the second overall pick, like Gordon two years earlier. Back in Little League, with Connie in the stands keeping score, Moustakas developed the skills and determination to make him a future big leaguer. His father Mike Sr. was his coach and mentor. "He kept motivating me and made me a better player," Moustakas said. "My dad is a competitor and he instilled that in me." In high school the young ballplayer gained national attention with his quick hands and power bat.

Moose continued to impress with big home run totals in the minors. Along with Hosmer, Kansas City promoted him from Omaha to the big league roster in the 2011 season. "They're both quality kids, in the clubhouse and outside the clubhouse," Yost said. "We know they're extremely talented but their makeup is off the charts for kids their age." Moustakas revealed his competitiveness and confidence even before he had ever played in a major league game. "We're about winning championships," he said, despite the Royals string of 90-loss seasons at the time.

After displaying solid power his first full year in the bigs, Moustakas slumped to .233/.287/.364 in 2013. The Royals nonetheless remained committed to him as their third baseman. He worked tirelessly to improve his fielding and hitting, impressing his coaches with his willingness to learn. "He's a kid that if you tell him to stand on his head and throw the ball over there, he'll stand on his head," said Mike Jirschele, Moose's manager at AAA Omaha. "So he takes instruction well and works his butt off."

Despite his work ethic and quick hands, Moustakas struggled in 2014. Batting just .152 in late May, the team demoted him to Omaha. When he returned to Kansas City after a short stint in the minors, his hitting improved but not by much. He finished the regular season with a career-low .212 batting average. But his resolve to get better and help his team win ballgames remained steadfast. In October he broke out, belting five home runs to set a franchise postseason record. He impressed with his glove as well. In Game 3 of the ALCS, for example, Moose made a highlight-reel catch falling into the dugout suite.

Heading into 2015, Moustakas was determined to build off his October success. Since opposing teams shifted their infielders to the right side when he batted, he worked on driving the ball to left. Hitting coach Dale Sveum helped him strip down his swing, so there was less movement from his body to get in the way of his quick, powerful hands. The reset worked. With Yost batting him second in the lineup, Moustakas became a hitting machine that targeted the entire field. Though his numbers dropped a bit after a torrid April, he entered the All-Star break with a productive .297/.353/.427 slash line. His 89 hits nearly matched his total from the entire 2014 regular season.

Off the field, Connie's health made 2015 a difficult season for Moustakas. Twice in the first half, he left the team on bereavement leave when his mother's condition declined. After the All-Star Game, Moose visited her in the hospital. He gave her his All-Star jersey, which brought a smile. Donning the shirt, Connie rallied, and her fighting spirit returned. "She was so proud that I was an All-Star," Moustakas said.

On Tuesday, July 14th, the American League and National League squared off in the 86th All-Star game at Great American Ball Park in Cincinnati. Angels slugger Mike Trout put the Junior Circuit up 1-0 with a leadoff home run. After the National

League tied it, Trout again scored in the fifth inning on a Prince Fielder single. Lorenzo Cain then drove in Albert Pujols with a double to extend the AL lead to 3-1. Wade Davis pitched a scoreless eighth inning, and the American League prevailed 6-3.

Cain contributed two hits and Escobar added one of his own in their team's victory. Perez went 0 for 2, striking out against Madison Bumgarner in a rematch of the last at-bat of the 2014 season. In his only at-bat, Moustakas struck out against Reds fireballer Aroldis Chapman. Herrera did not appear in the game.

The winner of the All-Star Game received home field advantage in the World Series. As with the year before, the American League champion would host Games 1 and 2 and Games 6 and 7 (if necessary) of the Fall Classic. In most seasons since Major League Baseball adopted the ASG World Series rule, home field advantage did not matter to Kansas City. But it certainly did in 2014. And with their team in first place in 2015, Royals fans hoped this All-Star Game result would again benefit their boys in the autumn.

PREPARING FOR OCTOBER

The Royals opened the second half of the season with four games in Chicago against the White Sox. The teams split the first two contests, a Friday double-header. Kansas City won a marathon third game when Cain hammered a thirteenth-inning homer. Danny Duffy shut down the Sox in the finale to give the Royals three of four at U.S. Cellular Field.

Returning home, Kansas City welcomed the Pirates for a three-game interleague series. Pittsburgh outslugged the Royals 10-7 in the opener. Giving up six runs in four innings, Ventura took the loss. After this pounding, the team demoted its struggling starter to Omaha, hoping he would regain his focus in a less stressful environment. Kansas City rebounded to capture the next two contests, limiting the Pirates to one run in each game.

The series victory, however, came with a price. Returning from the DL to start the second game against the Pirates, Jason Vargas threw only 26 pitches before left elbow pain ended his outing. An MRI revealed a torn ligament that would require Tommy John surgery. Kansas City lost a key member of its rotation for the rest of the season. To fill this absence, the team recalled Ventura just one day after sending him to the minors.

Traveling to St. Louis, the Royals dropped a 4-3 decision in a makeup of an earlier rainout. Back tightness hindered Royals starter Chris Young, who lasted only three innings against the Cardinals. The loss lowered the right-hander's record to 1-3 in his previous five starts. With Vargas out and Ventura and Young faltering, the clouds hovering above Kansas City's rotation grew darker.

The following night at Kauffman, Houston's Scott Kazmir, newly-acquired from Oakland, shut down the Royals while the Astro bats tagged Jeremy Guthrie for 11 hits. A top AL rival had thus improved its arm corps, while Kansas City's starting pitching looked even more desperate. Fortunately, Danny Duffy stopped the bleeding a night later, limiting the Astros to just one run over six innings. Kansas City prevailed with a walk-off RBI in the tenth from Escobar. The Royals then captured the finale when Ventura rebounded with seven strong innings to beat All-Star Game starter Dallas Keuchel.

Winning the Houston series was great news for Kansas City. And yet, defeating a potential playoff opponent was not even the best news of that day—Sunday, July 26. With MLB's trade deadline approaching, Dayton Moore completed a deal with Cincinnati for Reds starter Johnny Cueto. Kansas City had acquired a dominant top-of-the-rotation force, but the ace did not come cheaply. The Royals had to part with three promising lefty arms: John Lamb, Cody Reed, and Brandon Finnegan. The latter had pitched effectively in 2015 and the previous October, when he became the only player ever to appear in the College World Series and MLB World Series in the same year.

Johnny Cueto grew up in San Pedro de Macoris, a city on the southern coast of the Dominican Republic. Though his family avoided poverty, money was not plentiful. Cueto's mother Maria Christina raised him and his four siblings, while working long hours as a sales clerk. Cueto picked fruits and vegetables to help his mom, who made sure her children did not lack the essentials. For Johnny, this included a baseball, bat, and glove.

As a teenager, the short and skinny Cueto did not impress the big league scouts visiting his town. Johnny Almaraz of the Reds was the exception. Looking to find the next Pedro Martinez, an undersized Dominican pitcher who won three Cy Young awards, the Cincinnati scout gave the 18-year-old kid a tryout. Cueto impressed Almaraz with how fast the ball came out of his hand. "You knew he would throw harder when he got strong," Almaraz recalled, "but even then, he was 90-91 on the gun and he threw strikes." Cincinnati signed Cueto for $35,000.

Cueto debuted for the Reds in 2008, finishing 9-14 with a 4.81 ERA his rookie year. After a couple solid seasons, the right-hander missed starts in 2011 due to shoulder inflammation. Reds manager Dusty Baker sought to improve his pitcher's conditioning. "If you want to be a great pitcher ... you've got to stay on the hill," the manager told Cueto. Embracing this message, the pitcher adopted a rigorous cardio routine. Nearly every day between his starts, he jogged up the steps at the ballpark over and over. The hard work paid off. Cueto went 19-9 the following year, finishing fourth in the Cy Young voting.

Though a strained lateral muscle sidelined him for much of 2013, Cueto broke out better than ever in 2014. Mixing a 93-mph fastball with a beguiling array of curves, cutters, sliders, and change-ups, he won 20 games with a sparkling 2.25 ERA. These numbers earned him a second-place finish in the Cy Young voting. Known for his preparation and mound intelligence, he established himself as one of the league's top aces. Almaraz recalled that even in the minors, Cueto reviewed pitching charts, hitter by hitter. "He wanted to know location and

75

pitches and what happened on those pitches and how he could improve it," the scout said. Cueto added to his effectiveness by varying his windups, deliveries, and arm angles. This variety, including a pause-shimmy windup, added to his ability to throw off hitters' timing.

Cueto remained effective in the first half of the 2015 campaign. With the Reds out of contention and free agency looming at the end of the season, Cincinnati listened to trade offers. Dayton Moore sought a top ace that could bolster his team's battered rotation. With the Royals likely headed for the playoffs again, the GM wanted a starter who could go toe-to-toe against a Madison Bumgarner. Houston's acquisition of Scott Kazmir only increased this urgency. Moore found what he was looking for in the Cincy pitcher with the long dreadlocks. Cueto's reputation for joking around, moreover, made him a good fit for KC's laid-back clubhouse.

Royals Nation applauded Moore's big trade. Kansas City had significantly strengthened its roster for a title run.

The Royals next traveled to Cleveland, where they took the first two against the Tribe. The second victory featured perhaps the team's best defensive play of the year. In the ninth inning, Infante backhanded a grounder up the middle, then flipped it from his glove to Escobar, who barehanded the ball and fired to Hosmer for the out. The oft-replayed web gem helped preserve a one-run victory.

The Indians hammered Guthrie in the finale to avoid a sweep. While the Royals were in Ohio, their GM struck again with another trade deadline deal. On July 28, Moore acquired Ben Zobrist from Oakland for pitching prospects Aaron Brooks and Sean Manaea. The switch-hitting Zobrist brought a healthy .801 OPS and an ability to play the outfield and second base. Given Gordon's injury and the struggles of Alex Rios and Omar Infante, this acquisition made a lot of sense for Kansas City. If the team did not get the message before, they sure did now:

Dayton Moore wanted to win the World Series. And he wanted to win it in 2015.

Reporters by this time had noticed a strange new development with the Royals. Specifically, during interviews the players seemed to be fixated on the numbers 17 and 38. For example, Moustakas commented on a play by saying, "Hoz picks that thing 17 out of 38 times." Cain when asked to rank his team's top plays of the year said, "I mean all the plays we made all year … you can name 17 to 38 plays we've made all year." And so on. The origin of these numerical references was the song "Trap Queen," by rapper Fetty Wap. This song, used by Cain as his walk-up music before at-bats, includes in its lyrics a reference to Remy Martin 1738 cognac. The song became a team favorite to the point that the players starting fining each other if they did not work "1738" into an interview. As *Kansas City Star* reporter Andy McCullough noted, "Success has driven them mad."

The "mad" Royals traveled to Toronto to close out the month. Cooling off Yost's boys, the Blue Jays took the first two of a four-game set in Canada. Kansas City still finished July with a sterling 17-11 record. They were 20 games over .500 with an eight-game advantage in the AL Central. How things had changed since just a few years ago in Kansas City. Back then at the trade deadline, the team dealt away big-name players to contenders. Now the Royals were themselves contenders, adding star players for a World Series run.

Chapter 8

August: Accelerating

August began with the Royals in the midst of a four-game series in Toronto. After dropping the first two contests, Kansas City fell behind in the third game 5-1 after five innings. The Royal bats then woke up, plating three in the sixth and three more in the eighth, en route to a 7-6 victory. New acquisition Ben Zobrist homered from each side of the plate and scored three runs to spur the comeback. On the down side, Jose Bautista took Wade Davis deep in the eighth inning. It was the first home run allowed by the reliever in nearly two full years—back when Davis was a starter.

Tensions boiled over in the series finale. In the first inning Edinson Volquez hit Josh Donaldson on the left shoulder. The Blue Jay slugger, who had hit two homers and driven in seven thus far in the series, jawed with Volquez on his slow walk to first. When Donaldson batted in the third, the Royals pitcher again threw up and in, adding more fuel to the fire. Volquez had taken exception to Donaldson celebrating after his home runs in earlier games. "Somebody hits you, you've got to take it," Volquez later said, "because you're pimping everything you do." In the seventh, Royals reliever Ryan Madson hit Toronto shortstop Troy Tulowitzki and then buzzed Donaldson again. Incensed, the Blue Jays yelled at home plate umpire Jim Wolf, who ejected manager John Gibbons. An inning later, Toronto reliever Aaron Sanchez nailed Alcides Escobar in the thigh, prompting benches to empty. Wolf ejected Sanchez and Toronto coach DeMarlo Hale.

Though fired up, the Kansas City hitters could not solve Toronto knuckleballer R.A. Dickey, who pitched seven shutout innings. The Blue Jays prevailed 5-2, taking three of four in the contentious series. With four defeats in its last five contests, the Royals headed to Detroit.

Danny Duffy took the hill in the series opener against former Cy Young winner Justin Verlander. In his previous start, Duffy had allowed a career-high three home runs in a loss to the Blue Jays. This time the southpaw came through with a clutch performance, allowing just one run over seven innings. Kansas City picked up a much-needed 5-1 road win.

After his gem at Comerica Park, **Danny Duffy** finally seemed to be hitting his stride. Kansas City had won five of his previous six starts. The lefty's mid-summer emergence provided timely help for a rotation that had been racked with injury and ineffectiveness.

As a star pitcher at Cabrillo High in Lompoc, California, Duffy mowed down hitters with his mid-90s fastball. Despite concerns about wildness, Kansas City took the southpaw with its third pick in the 2007 draft. His talent was undeniable in the minors, but Duffy, as he himself admitted, had maturity issues as a young man. Some baseball evaluators even questioned his mental toughness. These concerns increased when Duffy left the Royals organization during spring training in 2010, citing a need to ponder whether he really wanted to play baseball.

After he returned three months later, team officials welcomed back their complicated hurler. Assistant general manager J.J. Picollo believed Duffy was misunderstood. "I think he cares almost too much at times," Picollo said. "And he expects so much out of himself, that it can work against him." The enigmatic southpaw pitched his way to AAA level in 2011.

After striking out 48 batters in just 42 innings in Omaha, Kansas City promoted him to The Show in May of that year. Just when it seemed Duffy would become a mainstay in the Royals rotation, disaster struck. Tearing an elbow ligament early in 2012, he required Tommy John surgery.

Faced with the worst crisis of his career, Duffy returned home to Lompoc, two-and-a-half hours north of Los Angeles. Running the nearby beaches eased his troubled mind. During the long months of rehabilitation and recovery, he gained maturity and perspective. Heading into the 2014 season, he was eager to contribute to the team in any role. "I just want to be part of the crew," he said.

The Royals placed Duffy in the bullpen at the start of the season, but an injury to starter Bruce Chen forced Yost to add him to the rotation. Duffy responded with a strong campaign. His 2.53 ERA led all Kansas City starters in 2014. In September, however, inflammation flared in his shoulder. Then in his last start, he suffered a cracked ribcage. This injury would limit him to just three relief appearances in the Royals' postseason run.

In the off-season, Duffy and Dave Eiland discussed a new conditioning program to improve the pitcher's durability. Working with strength and conditioning coach Ryan Stoneberg, Duffy focused on building his abdominal and leg muscles. He cut back on fast food and adopted a practical running program of two miles every other day. The younger Duffy, in contrast, binged on fast food and then burned it off with intense 10-mile mini-marathons.

Duffy reported to spring training in 2015 with more muscle mass in his core and legs. Yost commented that he had never seen the pitcher in better shape. Duffy hoped to log 200 innings, but biceps tendinitis in May knocked him out of the rotation. Returning from the DL in late June, he soon got back on track. After his victory in Detroit, Duffy's ERA dropped to 2.66 since recovering from his injury. Kansas City looked for more of the same from its lone southpaw starter in the stretch run.

Unfortunately the Royals could not maintain the momentum from their series-opening triumph in Detroit. In the second game, Matt Boyd outdueled Johnny Cueto to deliver a 2-1 win for the Tigers. The following day, Ian Kinsler hit a walk-off two-run homer in the ninth to give Detroit an 8-6 victory. After losing the series in Motown, Kansas City had dropped six of its last eight games. The Boys in Blue hoped to reverse this trend at The K, where they returned for a ten-game home stand. Though they remained in first place, a late summer collapse could still drop the team out of a playoff spot.

GUNS OF AUGUST

Opening the home stand, Edinson Volquez yielded just one run in seven innings to lift Kansas City to a 3-2 victory over the White Sox. The following evening was Husker Night at Kauffman Stadium. Legions of Nebraska fans trekked down I-29 to pick up a free Husker-KC cap and watch the Royals prevail 7-6. Though their favorite former Cornhusker did not play, the Big Red faithful received welcome news when Alex Gordon took batting practice for the first time since his injury a month earlier.

Sunday afternoon, the Royals made it three in a row over Chicago with a 5-4 victory. That evening Mike Moustakas found out that his mother Connie had died. His father told Mike that she had wanted him to "keep going out there, keep playing with the boys...." With a heavy heart, Moose reported for duty at the ballpark the next day. His teammates rallied around him. "Everybody somehow came to my side," Moustakas said, "picked me up when I was down and made sure I felt the love that everybody has on this team for me."

Detroit arrived for a three-game series. Making his home debut for the Royals, Johnny Cueto pitched a four-hit shutout in the first contest. The next night, Moustakas, Cain, and Hosmer each homered to extend Kansas City's winning streak to five. But Detroit erupted for 12 hits in the finale to avoid a sweep.

The home stand concluded with a four-game set against the Angels. Yost's boys had built a 5-1 lead heading into the eighth inning of the opener, when the inexplicable happened. The Halos shelled Wade Davis and Greg Holland with six runs (five earned) to pull out a 7-6 victory. The bullpen collapse marked the first time in 15 months that Kansas City had lost when leading after eight innings. Shaking off that head-scratching setback, the Royals took the next three from Los Angeles to complete an 8-2 home stand.

The series finale against the Angels featured an appearance from Kelvin Herrera, Wade Davis, and Greg Holland—KC's vaunted H-D-H bullpen trio. The relievers fared much better in that contest than they had in the series-opening disaster. When assessing the Royals' previous season success, the team had dominated in two areas: defense and bullpen. With each of the H-D-H boys finishing with a sub-1.50 ERA, the 2014 Kansas City relievers comprised arguably the best bullpen in baseball history. But H-D-H faced some unexpected road bumps in 2015 with Holland's DL stint, Herrera's suspension, and Davis's ailing back. The return of this rally-killing monster seemed a prerequisite for the team to get back to the World Series.

The youngest member of H-D-H, **Kelvin Herrera** represented yet another gem unearthed by Dayton Moore's revamped international scouting program. Growing up in Tenares, Dominican Republic, Herrera learned the value of hard work from his father Sebastian, a construction worker and former ballplayer. His mother Maria also helped young Kelvin stay focused on his baseball career. "Every time I got closer to my goal, my mother would encourage me not to get complacent," Herrera recalled. "She always said that you have to keep working hard to get the best out of yourself."

At age 16, Herrera grabbed the attention of Royals executive Rene Francisco and Latin American scouting coordinator Orlando Estevez during an informal throwing session after a tryout camp. Though scrawny, the kid displayed impressive arm quickness. After signing with Kansas City, Herrera emerged as a promising starter in the low minors. But the hard-throwing right-hander suffered an elbow stress fracture that sidelined him for nearly two seasons. Upon his return to action, the team shifted him to the bullpen. Herrera thrived in this new role. With a fastball that could hit 103 mph on the radar gun, he threw harder than any other Royal in franchise history. Developing a filthy change-up made the rookie a fixture in the KC pen in 2012. A loss of command, however, led to a regression in his sophomore year. After giving up a spate of home runs, the team sent him down to AAA Omaha. His month in the minors helped. Herrera returned to pitch effectively in the second half of the 2013 season.

Adding a curveball to his arsenal, Herrera emerged as one of the league's top relievers in 2014. By early summer, Yost gave him the seventh inning as his primary assignment. After the starter came out, Herrera's job was to shut down the opposition and hold the lead for the backend relievers. The dynamic right-hander excelled as the first head of the H-D-H monster. He posted a 1.41 ERA in 70 appearances and did not allow a home run the entire season. In the ALDS against Los Angeles, however, he had to exit Game 1 with arm tightness and numb fingers. After an MRI revealed no damage, Yost could again deploy this potent weapon. Herrera dominated in the ALCS, striking out six Orioles over 5 2/3 scoreless innings. In Game 7 of the World Series, he struck out four while keeping the Giants from scoring in two and two-thirds innings.

In 2015 the power reliever faced a couple of early-season setbacks when his homerless streak ended and he received a six-game suspension. Herrera nonetheless remained effective. With his ERA just over 2.00 at mid-season, Yost named him to the All-Star team. He immediately called his mother, just as he had done for each of his promotions through the Royals farm system. "I was sitting here, and I just can't believe it," Herrera said after receiving the news. "I'm so proud right now, to represent the Royals organization and Kansas City." As the 2015 season hit the stretch run, Yost could be confident that the seventh inning remained in good hands.

The H-D-H bullpen plan designated the eighth inning to **Wade Davis**. Heading into the 2014 season, Yost had penciled in Luke Hochevar as his primary setup man. But after Hochevar suffered a season-ending injury in spring training, Davis moved to the bullpen. The 6'5" right-hander deployed a devastating mix of high-90s fastballs, knuckling curves, and physics-defying cutters. The emotionless Davis presented such an intimidating Terminator-like presence, fans started to wonder if he actually was a cyborg designed by mad scientists to annihilate any batters in his path.

In an attempt to make Davis appear human, his lab-coated creators devised a backstory for him. According to this legend, Davis grew up in Lake Wales, a small town in central Florida. His mother Linda said that youth baseball coaches marveled at her son's ability to throw from the outfield to home plate. Eschewing football, Davis concentrated his athletic energies on baseball during his teen years. Following his completion of a stellar prep career, Tampa Bay drafted him in 2004.

After six years in the minors, Davis broke into the Rays rotation in 2010. He won 12 games as a rookie, plus Game 4 of the ALDS that year. After Davis turned in another decent season as a starter, manager Joe Maddon moved him to the bullpen for 2012. The right-hander adjusted well to the change, striking out 87 batters in just 70 innings.

In the off-season, Royals GM Dayton Moore looked to add a top-of-the rotation ace. He made a deal with the Rays, sending his top hitting prospect Wil Myers, highly-touted pitching prospect Jake Odorizzi, and a couple minor leaguers to Tampa Bay in exchange for James Shields and Davis. Though Shields was a solid starter, he had only two years left on his contract. Experts ripped Moore for giving up future stars like Myers and Odorizzi for such short-term returns. As for Davis, the middle reliever barely even registered in most assessments of the deal.

Kansas City's rivals responded with glee. Tigers writer Rob Rogacki called the trade a boneheaded mistake in which the Royals received just pennies on the dollar. "So rest easy, Tigers fans," Rogacki wrote, "and know that our divisional crown is in good hands with Royals GM Dayton Moore still at the helm."

Kansas City scribes were similarly unimpressed with the deal, though Davis did invite some curiosity. "It's unlikely that this trade will work out for the Royals," Rany Jazayerli wrote, "but if it does, Davis—not Shields—will be the key to the trade." With Kansas City's plan to move Davis back to the rotation, he would soon have the opportunity to vindicate Moore's transaction. Unfortunately, Davis struggled as a starter in 2013, posting a losing record and a 5.32 ERA. The trade thus appeared to be a "Royal Blunder," as Jazayerli called it.

Kansas City shifted Davis back to the bullpen for 2014. And then, deep within the bowels of Kauffman Stadium, the cyborg activated. Lacking a decent change-up, his Achilles heel as a starter, Davis developed a devastating cutter with late-breaking movement. Bulked up from spending hours in the gym with a personal trainer, Davis increased his fastball velocity. He destroyed batters in 2014, posting a 1.00 ERA in the regular season, while striking out 109 over 72 innings. His dominance continued in the postseason, when he allowed just one run in 14 1/3 innings. Like Herrera, he did not surrender a home run the entire year.

Davis somehow got even better in 2015. Over the first two months of the season, The Terminator did not allow a single earned run. In July he pitched in his first All-Star game. Back pain, however, slowed Davis in August. He missed some games and gave up a few runs. Was this just an aberration or was the cyborg breaking down?

There is good reason why teams trailing the Royals after eight innings had not won since May 2014. After running the Herrera-Davis gauntlet, opposing batters next had to face one of the game's most formidable closers. Over the two-season span of 2013-2014 **Greg Holland** saved 93 games, while posting a smothering 1.32 ERA. Abandon hope all ye who enter the ninth inning trailing the Royals.

A contrast from the towering Davis, the teenage Holland seemed an unlikely candidate to one day become baseball's most feared closer. While at McDowell High in Marion, North Carolina, the five-foot nothing, a hundred-and-nothing Holland instead bore more resemblance to Sean Astin in the movie *Rudy*. Prep coach Dennis "Flea" Blake recalled that Holland was not big enough or strong enough to pitch more than a few innings. "But he wanted to be a baseball player," Blake said, "loved to play, had a big ol' heart, and he had that drive, that determination." Inheriting pitching genes from his father Scott, who starred as a county team pitcher, and grandfather Ronald, who pitched in an industrial league, Greg kept at it. "He taught me a lot about the basic fundamentals of pitching," Holland said about his dad. Despite his determination, Holland's mid-80s fastball and control problems did not impress college recruiters. He showed more promise as a hitter, but still received no scholarship offers.

Undaunted, Holland enrolled at Western Carolina University and tried out for the baseball team as a walk-on. Though not the most talented player on the roster, the young right-hander impressed the Catamount coaches with his indefatigable work ethic. Growing bigger and stronger, as well as smarter about pitching, Holland attracted notice from pro scouts by his junior year. In 2007 Kansas City drafted him in the tenth round.

Holland made steady progress climbing the rungs of the Royals farm system ladder. Debuting in the majors in August 2010, however, the reliever struggled with a 6.75 ERA in 15 appearances. That winter, he played in Venezuela, where he improved his control and ability to put batters away. "When he came back from winter ball, he was a completely different pitcher," Yost said. "His command changed overnight." Holland, however, saw his improvement as part of a longer process. Over the years, he absorbed much wisdom from coaches and other players. Kansas City closers Joakim Soria and Jonathan Broxton, for example, taught him to stay with the moment as a reliever. "If you didn't get the last guy out," Holland said, "put it in the past and worry about getting the next guy out, then the next guy after that out."

When the Royals traded Broxton in the middle of the 2012 season, Holland took over as the team's closer. Not every skilled pitcher has the right mentality for the high-pressure job of closing out games. Hits, walks, and blown saves can shatter confidence. But Holland proved perfectly suited for this role. "He's very intense and has a great competitive spirit but he also shows great composure on the mound," Yost said. "Nothing rattles him."

Deploying a high-90s fastball and a filthy slider, Holland became a driving force in the Royals' October run in 2014. Posting a 0.82 ERA, he saved seven games in the postseason, including all four ALCS victories. But unbeknown to fans at the time, Holland had suffered ligament damage near the end of the regular season. He and the team hoped he would recover in the off-season and prosper again in 2015. But a strained pectoral sent him to the disabled list in April. A stiff neck then slowed him in May. As the summer went on, his fastball lost velocity and he blew saves. With his ERA approaching 4.00 in late August, he underwent an MRI. His elbow ligament was torn. Holland insisted he could still pitch. The Royals let him continue as closer. But as the team entered the home stretch, questions about Holland loomed more ominous.

ROYAL HEAT

Following their successful home stand, the Royals traveled to Cincinnati for a pair of games against the Reds. Much like a year earlier, the Boys in Blue turned up the heat in August. Kansas City took both games at Great American Ball Park to build another five-game winning streak.

The games at Cincinnati featured important contributions from less-heralded Royals relievers. Throughout the season, Yost had benefitted from the rise of four pitchers that had greatly improved his bullpen depth. In the opening game against the Reds, Franklin Morales and Kris Medlen each pitched scoreless frames in the thirteen-inning victory. After eight underwhelming years with the Red Sox and Rockies, Morales did not attract much attention when he signed with the Royals before the season. But a greater reliance on cutters and sinkers increased his ground ball rate. This, combined with pitcher-friendly park, resulted in a sub-3.00 ERA for Morales through mid-August. Kris Medlen won 15 games in 2013 as a promising starter for Atlanta. But when injury and Tommy John surgery shelved him for the 2014 season, the right-hander became expendable. Moore thought otherwise. Even though Medlen would not be available until midseason 2015, the GM believed he would regain his effectiveness and provide valuable depth for the Royals mound corps.

In the second game against the Reds, Luke Hochevar and Ryan Madson combined for two-and-two-thirds scoreless innings to help Kansas City preserve a 4-3 lead. The Royals' first-round draft pick in 2006, Hochevar endured five mediocre years as a starter before transitioning into an effective (1.92 ERA) reliever in 2013. A spring training injury, however, cost him the entire 2014 campaign. Hochevar struggled through a rocky first half in 2015, but displayed considerable improvement after the All-Star break. Longtime Phillies reliever Ryan Madson suffered an elbow ligament tear in 2012. After months of rehab and repeated failed tryouts, the right-hander retired from baseball. When Royals executive Jim Fregosi, Jr., asked him to tutor a high school prospect, Madson's interest in pitching rekindled. Dayton Moore gave him a chance, and Madson used a revitalized fastball and deceptive change-up to become an effective weapon in the KC bullpen.

Following the sweep in Cincinnati, the Royals found themselves in unfamiliar territory. They led the AL Central by 14.5 games with just a month and a half left in the season. A playoff berth was all but assured. Not since the 1980 team of George Brett, Willie Wilson, and Dennis Leonard had Kansas City built this sizeable of a lead in August. After their win over the Reds on the 19th, the Royals magic number dropped to 29.

Yost's boys flew to Boston for a four-game set at Fenway. The Red Sox unloaded 24 hits while taking the first two contests. Kansas City's new ace Cueto got shelled for six earned runs in the second loss. The Royals then returned the favor by pounding out 26 hits to take the next two games and split the series. In the finale, with the Royals down to their last out in the ninth trailing by two, Hosmer batted with the bases loaded. His clutch single to left tied the game. Two batters later, Moustakas hammered a double to drive in what proved to be the winning runs.

The Royals returned home to face Baltimore in a four-game set. For the opener, Yost picked Kris Medlen to take struggling Jeremy Guthrie's spot in the rotation. Making his first start in nearly two years, the right-hander surrendered just three runs in six innings to pick up the victory. Strong outings from Duffy and a resurgent Ventura gave Kansas City two of the next three and a series victory. In the Royals lone defeat to the Orioles, Cueto got battered again for six earned runs. Though disappointing on the mound thus far, the new acquisition seemed to be helping fellow Dominican Yordano Ventura turn his season around.

The Royals flew to Tampa Bay to close out the month with three games against the Rays. Kendrys Morales drilled a two-run homer to back a strong outing from Edinson Volquez in the opener. The next night, Moustakas delivered three hits and three RBIs to help the Royals win again. But Tampa Bay cooled the KC bats in the finale to avoid a sweep.

Kansas City finished August with a 19-9 record—the same mark Yost's boys had posted the previous August in their pennant-winning campaign. The Royals season record stood at

80-50. They led the division by a comfortable 13 games. And the good news did not end there: Alex Gordon had returned to the field, playing rehabilitation games in Omaha. The best left fielder in the league would soon rejoin his team.

Chapter 9

September: Magic Numbers

September 1st was an eventful day for the Royals. The Boys in Blue returned to The K to open a nine-game home stand. The team honored its Franchise Four. And Kansas City announced its September call-ups.

Each season Major League Baseball allows teams to expand their rosters from 25 to 40 players at the beginning of September. With minor league seasons ending, top prospects gain opportunities to compete at the big league level. Roster expansion also allows contending teams to bolster their lineups with young talent for a late-season push.

Kansas City's most significant call-up was not a minor leaguer, but rather a veteran leader. On September 1st, the Royals officially activated Alex Gordon. After a week of rehab games with Omaha, the star left fielder rejoined his team for the first time in nearly two months. Yost inserted him in the six-spot in his lineup for that evening's game.

The Royals also welcomed outfielder Jonny Gomes, whom Dayton Moore had acquired from Atlanta for cash and infield prospect Luis Valenzuela. Gomes brought a veteran bat and World Series experience to his new team. As for minor leaguers, Kansas City promoted highly-touted pitching prospect Miguel Almonte and southpaw reliever Scott Alexander. Pinch-running specialist Terrance Gore, a 2014 postseason hero, also joined the Royals. Other call-ups included catcher Francisco Pena and infielders Cheslor Cuthbert and Christian Colon. A first-round draft pick in 2010, Colon etched his name in franchise lore by scoring the winning run in the 2014 Wild Card game. He had batted .244 for Kansas City in limited action earlier in 2015.

Prior to the September 1st contest against the Tigers, the Royals honored their Franchise Four. Earlier in the season, fans nationwide voted for their team's all-time top four players, a baseball version of Mount Rushmore for each franchise. The top four Royals were: George Brett (3B), a Hall of Famer and the best player in team history; Frank White (2B), an eight-time Gold Glove winner and 1980 ALCS MVP; Bret Saberhagen (P), a two-time Cy Young winner and 1985 World Series MVP; and Dan Quisenberry (P), the premier closer of his day who led the league in saves five times. Brett, White, Saberhagen, and Janie Quisenberry Stone, Dan's widow, threw out ceremonial first pitches before the game.

The Tigers unfortunately dampened the festive occasion. Powered by 11 hits, the visitors edged the Royals 6-5. To make matters worse, the team learned that it would be without two key players when Kelvin Hererra and Alex Rios were diagnosed with chicken pox. Kansas City sent both players home to keep the contagious illness from infecting their teammates. It would be a week before Herrera and Rios returned to action.

The rest of the team fortunately showed no ill-effects. In the next two games, KC batters destroyed Tiger pitching with 34 hits and 27 runs to take the series in dominating fashion. But the Kauffman guns ran out of ammo when the White Sox arrived. Chicago outscored the Royals 25-7 in a three-game sweep.

On Labor Day, Minnesota extended Kansas City's losing streak to four. That matched the team's longest skid of the year. The next night, Eric Hosmer and Kendrys Morales combined for four first-inning RBIs to move the Royals back to the winning column. The Twins, however, claimed the rubber game 3-2 in twelve innings.

Despite the defeat, Kansas City hit a milestone in the final game of the home stand. That night the Royals set a franchise record for home attendance in a season. The previous mark of 2,477,700 dated back to 1989. Averaging more than 33,400 fans per game in 2015 (fourth best in the AL), Kansas City had six more home dates to add to its record.

In the tenth inning of the series finale against Minnesota, **Jarrod Dyson**, pinch running for Ben Zobrist, stole second and third with just one out. Though he was thrown out at the plate on Cain's chopper to the mound, Dyson's dual thefts showcased his proficiency on the base paths. "That's what speed do," as he would say. But the swift outfielder, nicknamed Mr. Zoombya, was far more than just a baserunning specialist. Following Gordon's injury in early July, Dyson stepped up to provide timely hits and key defensive plays to help the Royals continue rolling. Gordon himself noted his replacement's contributions. "He brings a lot of excitement to the game and he's probably the best backup outfielder in the game," Alex said.

Growing up in McComb, Mississippi, Dyson dreamed about one day winning the World Series. But the youngster faced significant obstacles to realizing that dream. Drug dealers roamed his neighborhood, and gun shots occasionally rang out. Dyson's slight build also did not seem conducive to any athletic aspirations. He quit playing baseball during his middle school years—a decision he later regretted. Returning to the diamond in high school, Dyson brought phenomenal speed and a defiant determination to the field. After graduation, he moved on to Southwest Mississippi Community College.

The undersized ballplayer at a small community college attracted little attention from pro scouts. But he did catch the eye of Brian Rhees of the Royals. The scout raved about Dyson to his supervisor Junior Vizcaino, who showed up at a game and graded the kid's speed as an *80*—the top score on a scout's scale for rating player abilities. Vizcaino urged KC scouting director

Deric Ladnier to take a flier on the speedster, which he did with the team's 50th-round pick in the 2006 draft.

Dyson struggled at the plate in the low minors, limiting his playing time. The team came very close to cutting him, but KC officials remained intrigued with his speed. "He was showing improvement," said assistant GM J.J. Picollo. "And he had that tool that we just didn't have in our system." The Royals stuck with Dyson, and his batting average rose. He got his first taste of The Show in 2010 as a September call-up. Though he spent most of the following season back in the minors, an injury to Lorenzo Cain returned him to the big leagues in 2012. He stole 30 bases in a hundred games that season, and 34 more as a fourth outfielder the following year.

In 2014 Dyson became an even more valuable contributor to the Royals. In addition to his role as a top reserve outfielder and pinch runner, Yost commonly inserted Mr. Zoombya into games as a defensive replacement for right fielder Nori Aoki. Dyson helped solidify one of the best fielding outfields in baseball, while contributing a .269 batting average, 36 stolen bases, and 120 games (all career highs) to the AL pennant winners.

With a mouth constantly on the move, Dyson's quips, putdowns, and boasts helped keep the clubhouse loose. He relished these contributions. "Y'all stay focused," he told his teammates during the 2014 ALCS. "I'll do the talking." Though sometimes ruffling opposition feathers, his daily bragging elevated the Royals. "He's probably the most confident person I've been around," said Eric Hosmer. "Hanging out with him, that confidence rubs off on you."

A groin injury slowed Dyson early in the 2015 season. He was batting just .219 at the end of May, but the hits came in greater frequency that summer when he was called upon to replace Gordon. On the day of Alex's injury, Dyson gunned down a baserunner and hit an inside-the-park home run. He topped out at 21.5 mph while rounding the bases. Heading into the home stretch of the season, Dyson continued to show the world what speed could do.

CLINCHING

On Friday, September 11th, the Royals arrived in Baltimore to begin a ten-game road trip. Kansas City led 6-4 in the opener heading into the bottom of the eighth. A lead that late pretty much always ended in a Royals victory. But then came an inning of unimaginable horrors for the KC bullpen. With Herrera on the mound, Baltimore loaded the bases with two hits and a KC error. Making the most of this opportunity, Oriole outfielder Nolan Reimold launched a drive that hit high off the left field foul pole. Herrera, who did not allow a home run in all of 2014, had given up a grand slam. Yost brought in Franklin Morales, who surrendered a homer and an RBI double. Yost summoned reliever Joba Chamberlain, who had been called up from Omaha a few days earlier. Alex Gordon's former Cornhusker teammate walked the bases loaded and then served up a home run to Steve Clevenger. So the most dominant bullpen in baseball gave up two grand slams and 10 runs in a single inning. With Kansas City's sixth loss in seven games, concerns about a late season collapse spread across Royals Nation.

Mike Moustakas revived his flagging team the next day. Lowering his antlers, Moose gored the Orioles with a two-run single, a grand slam, and a three-run homer. The nine-RBI game set a new franchise record. "It's pretty special," the third baseman said. "I was just able to get good pitches, and I didn't miss them today."

In the series finale, Baltimore shelled Johnny Cueto, tagging him with his fifth straight loss. Over that span, the Royals highly-prized pitching acquisition had surrendered 28 earned runs in 26 1/3 innings. Kansas City still maintained a ten-game lead in the division, but with the decline of their top ace and recent bullpen meltdown, the team did not looked destined for October glory.

The Royals traveled to Cleveland, where they staunched the bleeding somewhat by splitting four games with the Indians. In the first of the two wins, Kris Medlen delivered his best outing of the year to help stabilize a collapsing rotation. In KC's other win in Cleveland, Omar Infante channeled his inner Moose to drive in seven runs. For the second baseman, who had been benched for most of September, the outburst provided hope for a late season turnaround.

Traveling to Detroit for the final leg of the road trip, the Royals absorbed two significant injury blows. Leading 4-3 heading into the bottom of the twelfth, Yost brought in Holland to finish off the win. The closer instead allowed three hits and two runs for his fifth blown save of the year. It would be the last time Holland pitched this season. Aware from an August MRI of an elbow ligament tear, the right-hander had tried to pitch through the pain. He recorded three saves in September to up his season total to 32, but by the middle of the month it became evident that the injury was too severe. The team needed to shut Holland down. He would have Tommy John surgery a couple weeks later.

Holland was not the only Royal whose season ended in Detroit. Suffering an oblique strain in the series opener against the Tigers, Omar Infante headed to the trainer's room. The injury, later diagnosed as a Grade 1 strain, would prevent Infante from playing again in 2015. Ben Zobrist, who was already starting ahead of Infante on most days, would play second base the rest of the season.

Detroit claimed another extra-inning walk-off victory in the second contest, before Kansas City unloaded 19 hits in the finale to avoid a sweep. Leading the charge in that Motor City eruption, Kendrys Morales slammed three homers and a triple to set a franchise record with 15 total bases. The Royals returned to The K to face Seattle. Unfortunately, the Mariners exploded for 13 hits and 11 runs to blow out the home team in the opener.

The starter in that dismal game, **Jeremy Guthrie**, gave up eight runs in just two and one-third innings against Seattle. It was yet another rough outing for the right-hander, who had struggled to a 5.95 ERA on the season. A mainstay in the Kansas

City rotation since mid-2012, Guthrie had made his last start for the 2015 Royals.

From his youthful days of hitting tee-ball home runs into a neighbor's pool, Guthrie seemed destined for athletic greatness. He starred in three sports in high school, playing quarterback, point guard, and pitcher/third base for his prep teams. As if that were not enough, the star athlete flexed his cerebral muscle by graduating as valedictorian.

After a disappointing college freshman season pitching for Brigham Young, Guthrie spent the next two years in Spain on a Mormon mission. Returning to the States, he enrolled at Stanford University, where he earned Pac-10 Pitcher of the Year honors as a junior. In June 2002 Cleveland selected him with its first-round draft pick.

Guthrie failed to dazzle Indians officials during his four years in their farm system. The Orioles claimed him off waivers in 2007. Guthrie proved a durable starter in Baltimore, topping 190 innings four straight seasons. But he also lost more games than he won. In February 2012 the Orioles traded him to Colorado, where he struggled at the hitters' paradise known as Coors Field. In July the Rockies traded him to the Royals for Jonathan Sanchez, an equally disappointing starter.

With a pitcher-friendly park and Gold Glove-caliber defenders behind him, Guthrie revived his career in Kansas City. From mid-2012 through the end of 2014, he posted a 33-26 record with a 3.92 ERA. Though not an ace, he remained a valuable innings-eater, topping 200 frames in both 2013 and 2014. He won Game 3 of the World Series and started Game 7 against the Giants.

Guthrie began 2015 winning four of his first six decisions. But after the Yankees riddled him with 11 earned runs on Memorial Day, Guthrie never fully righted his ship. Though his fastball still topped 90-mph, he lost the command that he had relied upon in past seasons. Yost removed him from the rotation in August, before giving him one more start in September. After the Seattle debacle, he left the rotation for good.

Though Guthrie would no longer contribute on the mound, he remained an influential veteran presence for the Royals. He promoted chess in the clubhouse and served as an interpreter for Spanish-speaking teammates. During Kansas City's drive to the 2014 pennant, he had proved an enthusiastic leader of his team's postgame celebrations. He continued this role in 2015, hoping the season would end with the biggest clubhouse party of them all.

With a 7-13 mark since the start of the month, September had not gone well for the Royals. But their closest pursuers in the division, the Twins, had not fared much better. Minnesota had gained only two games on Kansas City since September 1st. As the Royals prepared to host the Mariners on September 23rd, their division lead was still 10 games. After Lorenzo Cain drove home the winning run in the tenth inning that evening, Kansas City's magic number dropped to two.

The following night, in the series finale, the Royals unleashed a 15-hit barrage to overpower the Mariners 10-4. That victory, combined with Minnesota's loss to Cleveland, clinched the AL Central for the Boys in Blue. It was the team's first division title since 1985. Yost danced in the dugout. Duffy donned a bear suit. The players sprayed each other with champagne in the clubhouse, before Dyson led his teammates back onto the field to salute the jubilant fans remaining in the stadium.

During the postgame celebration, owner David Glass recalled the preseason predictions for his team: "The experts said we were going to win 72 games. And we did. A long time ago." Yost noted the contrast between this achievement and clinching the wild card a year earlier. "It's a different kind of feeling," the manager said. "It's something I've expected from the first day of spring training." His eyes burning from champagne, Cain looked to the road ahead. "We understand that we're not done," the centerfielder said. "We've got a lot of unfinished business to take care of."

In the division-clinching victory, **Ben Zobrist** contributed two doubles and scored three runs. Moore acquired the versatile utility player at the end of July to provide outfield depth while Alex Gordon was still on the DL. With Omar Infante out for the year, Zobrist became Kansas City's everyday second baseman and the number-two batter in Yost's lineup.

Though one of the newest Royals, Zobrist had Kansas City connections that dated back more than three decades. His father Tom had attended Calvary Bible College in KC, before moving to Eureka, Illinois, where Ben was born. The pastor at Eureka's Liberty Bible Church, Tom drove his family to Kansas City to attend games at Royals Stadium. As a toddler in the early 1980s, Ben wore a Royals T-shirt with his name and the number "1" on the back.

Growing up, Zobrist displayed a competitive drive to succeed. Adopting a rigorous fitness routine that included hundreds of push-ups and sit-ups, he developed a physique that allowed him to run a 5:01 mile as a seventh-grader. In the backyard, he built a Wiffle ball field with painted baselines, lights, and an outfield fence. Tom believes that backyard field is where Ben learned to switch hit and play multiple positions.

Though he played varsity baseball all four years in high school, Zobrist received no scholarship offers. His athletic career seemingly over, Ben planned to attend his dad's alma mater to become a youth pastor. He then learned about a tryout camp where college coaches evaluated high school seniors. Tom thought the $50 fee a waste, but allowed his son to use birthday money from his grandparents to pay for it. After displaying his skills at the tryout, Zobrist received a scholarship offer to play for Olivet Nazarene, a nearby NAIA Christian college. Though his mother Cindi worried that baseball would prevent her son from following his true calling in the ministry, she and Tom trusted their son to make the best decision for himself. After much prayer, Zobrist felt that God was leading him to play baseball.

Following three successful years at Olivet Nazarene, Zobrist transferred to Dallas Baptist University to compete against Division I players. After a strong senior season, the Astros selected Zobrist in the sixth round of the 2004 draft. Two years later, Houston traded the promising prospect to Tampa Bay. Promoted to the majors soon after the trade, Zobrist struggled to hit big league pitching. He bounced between the minors and Tampa Bay in 2007-2008. By this time Zobrist made his off-season home in Nashville, where his wife Julianna was launching her career as a Christian music artist. While in Tennessee he had a chance meeting with hitting instructor Jamie Cevallos, who helped the switch-hitter improve his stance and swing. At the same time, Ben bulked up his size and strength.

The new and improved Zobrist delivered his best season yet in 2009 with a .297 average, 27 homers, and 91 RBIs. Making the All-Star team and finishing in the top ten in AL MVP voting, he acquired the nickname Zorilla for his newfound power. After a down year in 2010, Zobrist delivered two more 20-homer seasons for the Rays, and again made the All-Star team in 2013. In January 2015, Oakland GM Billy Beane traded for the super utility man.

A medial meniscus tear in his left knee required Zobrist to undergo arthroscopic surgery in late April. He returned after a month and put up strong numbers in June and July. But when the A's fell out of the contention by midseason, they fielded trade offers. Moore jumped at the opportunity to add Zobrist. In addition to his versatility, the veteran ballplayer brought yet another positive influence to the Kansas City clubhouse. Former Rays teammate Ben Shouse noted that Zobrist looked for ways to encourage those around him. "Ben is the kind of player you would want on your team," Shouse said, "... he plays hard, he wants to learn and improve, and he has a great attitude." Yost appreciated Zobrist's ability to get on base and create RBI opportunities. "With Omar going down, he's filled in at second base great," the manager said. "And his offense has been key from both sides of the plate."

HOME FIELD ADVANTAGE

Even with a playoff spot assured, the division-champion Royals still had work to do in the regular season. With 10 games left, Kansas City led Toronto by just two games for the best record in the American League. Keeping this top seed would ensure home field advantage if the teams faced each other in the ALCS. As the hottest club in baseball the past seven weeks, the Blue Jays loomed as the biggest obstacle to the Royals' quest to return to the World Series. Barely above .500 at the end of July, Toronto ripped off 11 straight wins in August to finish the month at a blistering 21-6. The Jays remained hot in September and seemed likely to overtake the flagging Royals for home field advantage.

The day after clinching the division, Yost rested most of his regulars for the game against Cleveland. Indians starter Carlos Carrasco destroyed the Royals B-Team, striking out 15 while tossing a one-hit shutout. The next night, the Tribe pounded out 12 hits to drop another defeat on Yost's boys. Since Toronto won again, the Blue Jays caught the Royals for best record in the AL. While losing home field advantage was not the end of the world (the 2014 Royals did not need it), playing the surging Blue Jays at Kauffman was preferable to facing them in Canada—especially with the opposite trajectories the teams were on in September.

In the series finale in Cleveland, Chris Young and the Royals bullpen shut out the Tribe. Though his father Charles had died a day earlier, Young insisted on taking the mound to honor him. "I felt him next to me with every pitch," Young said. His manager noted the difficult circumstances of that outing. "To go out with that on his heart and throw five innings of no-hit baseball was unbelievable," Yost said.

The Royals would play their final seven regular season games on the road. Travelling to Chicago, Yost's boys stopped at Wrigley Field to play a makeup of a game rained out earlier in the season. The pitching-dominated contest entered the eleventh inning as a scoreless tie. In the bottom of the frame, pinch-hitter

Chris Denorfia homered off Miguel Almonte to deliver a Cubs victory.

Remaining in the Windy City, the Royals headed to the South Side for three games against the White Sox. Their old nemesis Jeff Samardzija outpitched Cueto in the opener to send Kansas City to its fourth loss in five games. The team trailed Toronto by a game and a half for best record in the American League. With just five games remaining, home field advantage appeared to have slipped away. The next night, Hosmer hit a two-run homer in the tenth to propel Kansas City to victory. The Royals finished September at 11-17—the team's first losing month since July 2014. The following evening, October 1st, Kris Medlen pitched six strong innings, and Jonny Gomes drove in three to give KC the finale in Chicago. With three games left, Kansas City and Toronto had identical 92-57 records.

The Royals traveled to Minnesota for their final series of the regular season. Recapturing their August prowess, Yost's boys outscored the home team 14-3 in the three contests at Target Field to finish with an impressive sweep and a five-game winning streak. With Toronto dropping its last two games at Tampa Bay, Kansas City reclaimed the American League's best record. Hosmer commented that gaining home field advantage was important. "We're built for our ballpark as a team," the first baseman said. "What the fans do for us, the way they make the atmosphere there, it makes it tough for opposing teams to come in."

Both Ventura and Cueto pitched well in Minnesota to win their final regular season starts. Ventura finished the season winning nine of his last 10 decisions, providing hope that he had finally righted the ship. Cueto turned in his fourth decent outing in a row, assuaging some of the fears that he would be a postseason liability. This turnaround for Cueto came after he had asked Salvador Perez to hold his mitt lower. This improved the pitcher's optics, making him less likely to leave his change-ups and cutters high in the zone where batters could feast on them.

A change on offense also contributed to the Royals late-season rebound. Weeks earlier, Yost had moved Alcides Escobar out of the leadoff spot in his lineup. The free-swinging shortstop had an OBP of .260 since the All-Star break—subpar for a leadoff man and about 100 points below that of Gordon and Zobrist. Following the change, Kansas City dropped nine of its next 16 games. After Yost moved Escobar back to the leadoff spot on September 30th, the Royals won their last five games of the season. Sabermetric research mandates that a batting order must include a high-OBP hitter at the top. But when Escobar and his below average .293 OBP led off in 2015, his team was 82-49. When he did not lead off, the Royals were just 13-18. The reasons for this defied statistical explanation. Moore attributed the phenomenon to team chemistry and psychology. Hosmer agreed, stating that the team felt more comfortable with Escobar leading off. Yost had no theory. "Again, that's a mystery to all of us," the manager said, "but it works."

There would be no mystery about who would be leading off for Kansas City in the 2015 playoffs.

Chapter 10

American League Division Series

Entering their second consecutive postseason, Ned Yost and his boys were ready for October baseball. "I'm glad we're done with the marathon, the 162," the manager said. "Now the fun starts." To kick off the fun, the Royals hosted a "Take the Crown" rally at Kauffman Stadium. Similar to a year earlier, about 5,000 fans showed up at The K to watch their favorite players up close during a batting practice turned pep rally. Many of those in attendance had skipped work or classes to join the festivities at the ballpark.

On the eve of the American League Division Series, ESPN aired a new *30 for 30* short titled, *#BringBackSungWoo*. The documentary covered the efforts of filmmakers Josh Swade and Josh Shelov to convince the bosses of SungWoo Lee to allow the South Korean Royals fan to return to Kansas City for the 2014 World Series.

As the hours ticked away before the first pitch of the ALDS, Royals fan enthusiasm reached a fever pitch—just as it had before the Wild Card game a year earlier. But this time, the KC faithful had higher hopes. "My expectations for them are that they win it all," said Ryan Land of Lee's Summit, expressing a common sentiment in western Missouri. Some fans believed the Royals' stronger offense was the difference-maker that would put them over the top. "Last year they didn't have the power that we have this year," said season ticket holder Rick Evans. Other fans, such as Topeka's Amanda Cross, pointed to experience as a key factor. "I think this team will be less nervous going into the postseason," Cross said, "because they now know what to expect."

The Royals held another advantage over their first-round playoff opponent. As division champions, Kansas City avoided the winner-take-all Wild Card game played just two days after the end of the regular season. The teams squaring off in that contest would have to use their top aces, while the Royals could rest their pitchers. The American League wild card qualifiers were the Houston Astros and the New York Yankees. The Astros prevailed 3-0 in the Bronx to advance to face Kansas City.

Though they had won nine fewer regular season games than the Royals, the Astros posed a formidable challenge. Boasting five power hitters with 20-plus home runs, the Houston lineup bristled with heavy artillery. Pitching ace Dallas Keuchel posted an AL-best 20 wins and a 2.48 ERA—numbers that made him a lock to win the Cy Young Award. Houston's staff also included 19-game winner Collin McHugh and Scott Kazmir, the team's big mid-season acquisition.

Perhaps even more troubling from the Royals point of view was the narrative the Astros brought into the postseason. After a string of losing seasons, Houston entered 2015 projected to finish below .500. Led by A.J. Hinch, a former catcher with a losing record as a manager, the team shocked the baseball world by remaining in contention the entire season. After ending a long playoff drought, Houston scored an upset victory in the Wild Card game. And now this group of hungry underdogs sought to blaze a path through the AL playoffs. The 2015 Astros thus looked remarkably similar to the 2014 Royals, who swept away Los Angeles (the team with the league's best record) in the ALDS.

Statistics did little to assuage the anxiety of KC fans hoping to avoid the fate of the 2014 Angels. While the Royals hit for a higher average (.269 to .250), Houston's power-laden lineup slugged 91 more homers. Stolen bases also favored the Astros 121 to 104. On the pitching side, Houston led the AL with a 3.57 ERA, while Kansas City finished third with a 3.73 mark. Despite the loss of Greg Holland, the Royals still boasted the better bullpen. Houston's relievers, however, were not far behind statistically speaking.

Houston had won four of six regular season meetings with the Royals. But Kansas City fans could find optimism in the Wild Card factor. Since Keuchel had just pitched against the Yankees, he could start only one game in the best-of-five ALDS.

Experts predicted a close series. Johnny Cueto represented the X-factor—would Good Johnny or Bad Johnny show up in the playoffs? In a short series, the answer to that question could prove decisive.

ALDS GAME 1

Yost tabbed Yordano Ventura to start the first game of the Royals 2015 postseason. The young right-hander had come a long way since spring. Uneasy bearing the mantle of staff ace, he struggled early in the season. His composure disintegrated in April, when he incited three bench-clearing incidents. An ulnar nerve inflammation sent him to the disabled list in June, keeping him off the mound for nearly a month. When he returned in July, opposing batters teed off on his deliveries. But over the final two months of the season, Ventura recaptured the dominant form he had displayed during his rookie campaign. In his last eleven starts he posted a 2.38 ERA, with 81 strikeouts in 68 innings. This turnaround came after Ventura harnessed command of his curves and change-ups. "When he's got that secondary pitch for a strike," Salvador Perez said, "then he's going to be great."

Astros manager A.J. Hinch countered with Collin McHugh. A workhorse during the regular season, the right-hander went

19-7 with a 3.89 ERA in 200-plus innings. Like Ventura, he gained momentum in the stretch run. Riding an elite curveball and a hard-breaking cutter, McHugh posted a 2.89 ERA after August 1st.

Julianna Zobrist sang the national anthem before Game 1. The Christian singer was due to release her third album in a few days. At eight months pregnant, she was also due to soon welcome her third child with husband Ben. The Royals selected World War II Army veteran Hugh "Coach" Dunn to throw out the ceremonial first pitch. After Dunn, a Purple Heart recipient and member of the Missouri Coaches Hall of Fame, fired in a strike, the Royals took the field.

With rain clouds hovering above The K, Houston did not waste any time going on the attack. A single, a walk, and another single loaded the bases for the Astros with nobody out in the top of the first. Back-to-back groundouts from left fielder Colby Rasmus and designated hitter Evan Gattis plated two runs for the visitors. Ben Zobrist singled and stole a base in the bottom of the frame, but Kansas City could not answer.

In the second, Jake Marisnick, Houston's number-nine hitter, lined a double into left center. Second baseman Jose Altuve then singled him home to extend the Astros lead. The Royals got the run back in the bottom of the frame, when Kendrys Morales drilled a McHugh fastball into the right field seats. The rain then picked up, forcing the umpires to call for the tarp. The break lasted 49 minutes, convincing Yost to replace Ventura with Chris Young. Since the delay did not exceed an hour, Hinch left McHugh in the game.

Following a scoreless third, Morales took McHugh deep again in the fourth. The 414-foot blast to right cut the Astros lead to 3-2. It marked the first multi-homer postseason game for a Royal since George Brett's offensive explosion in Game 3 of the 1985 ALCS. Houston, however, answered in its next at bat when right fielder George Springer deposited a Young delivery into the seats in left center.

McHugh allowed a single to Alex Gordon and a walk to Alex Rios in the bottom of the fifth, but Kansas City could not capitalize. The Houston starter breezed through a one-two-three sixth, and reliever Tony Sipp sent the Royals down in order in the seventh. In the top of the eighth, Rasmus launched a bomb off Ryan Madson to extend the margin to 5-2. Zobrist and Cain singled in the bottom half of the frame, but again the Royals could not break through.

Needing just three more outs, Hinch brought in his closer Luke Gregerson for the ninth. The right-hander had saved 31 games during the regular season, while averaging nearly a strikeout per inning. Morales led off, looking to match George Brett as the only Royal to homer three times in one postseason game. Gregerson struck him out. The reliever then hit Mike Moustakas, giving KC a baserunner and a glimmer of hope for a comeback. But Perez went down swinging and Gordon fouled out to end the game.

After just one contest, Kansas City had already lost more games in the AL playoffs than a year earlier. "It's a five-game series," Yost said. "It's not a death sentence to lose Game 1." But the setback put the Royals in a difficult position. Ace Dallas Keuchel awaited them in Game 3 in Houston, where he did not lose a single decision in 2015. If they could not turn things around in Game 2, the Boys in Blue would face the prospect of an early exit from the postseason.

ALDS GAME 2

The starting pitchers for the second game of the ALDS were Johnny Cueto and Scott Kazmir. These hurlers had traveled similar roads to arrive at this contest. Acquiring Kazmir from Oakland in a mid-season trade, Astros GM Jeff Luhnow hoped the 15-game winner from 2014 would strengthen his team's rotation for a deep run in the postseason. But the three-time All-Star struggled in Houston, posting a 2-6 record after the trade. He went winless in September with a 6.52 ERA. On the bright side for Astros fans, the southpaw had pitched effectively in his three starts against Kansas City in 2015.

Like Kazmir, Cueto found himself traded to a contender in July. And similar to Kazmir, Cueto disappointed with his new team. The former Cincinnati ace posted a 4-7 record and a 4.76 ERA with the Royals. Such numbers could be forgiven and forgotten though. Kansas City had the division locked up by August and did not need Cueto to contribute much for the stretch run. Dayton Moore acquired him to win big games in October. If he did that, the trade would be a success.

As the Royals took the field for Game 2, their fans hoped that ace Johnny would show up that afternoon. But trouble came right out of the gate when the right-hander walked Springer and allowed an RBI-double to Rasmus in the top of the first. The situation worsened in the second when Houston loaded the bases with nobody out. After a shallow fly out, Springer fisted a blooper into left to plate two more runs. With his team down 3-0, Salvador Perez struck back with a solo homer in the bottom of the second. But the Astros got the run back their next at-bat when Rasmus blasted a shot over the wall in right center. Fans throughout the quieted ballpark pondered what was wrong with Cueto. Having allowed four runs in three innings, the prize acquisition from Cincy looked like one of the biggest trade busts in franchise history.

Undaunted by the early deficit, the Royals continued battling. An Alex Rios double and a bunt single from Alcides Escobar placed runners at the corners with no outs in the third. Zobrist followed with a double-play grounder. Though not an ideal result, Kansas City plated a run to cut the Houston lead to two.

Despite his starter's rocky first three innings, Yost left Cueto in the game. With the faith of his manager, the dreadlocked one had a chance to limit the damage and keep his team in the game. And that is exactly what he did. Cueto prevented Houston from scoring over the next three innings, allowing only a walk in the fifth and a single in the sixth.

Kazmir, however, got into a groove as well. The southpaw posted zeros in the fourth and fifth innings. Heading into the bottom of the sixth, Kansas City still trailed by two in a game it had to win. With one out, Lorenzo Cain laced a double into the right field corner. Hinch pulled his starter for Oliver Perez. Eric Hosmer fell behind 0-2 against the southpaw, before lunging with his bat to drop a flare into left center that scored Cain. Following this "booty knock" (term coined by Rex Hudler), a Morales single and a Moustakas walk loaded the bases. Hinch brought in Josh Fields to face Salvador Perez. The free-swinging catcher had walked only 13 times during the regular season. But Salvy took four straight offerings outside the zone to draw a base on balls. Hosmer trotted home with the tying run.

With the score knotted 4-4 heading to the seventh, the game became a battle of the bullpens. Advantage: Kansas City. After Kelvin Herrera sent the Astros down with only a benign single, Houston's Will Harris came on to pitch the bottom of the seventh. Escobar tagged him with a triple into the gap in right center. Zobrist followed by slapping an RBI-single into left. Kansas City led 5-4.

Ryan Madson retired the Astros in order in the eighth. Yost summoned Wade Davis for the ninth. Recovering from back pain that had hindered him in August, the reliever returned to form in September after taking over Greg Holland's closer role. But The Terminator opened the door for Houston with a one-out walk to Preston Tucker. Hinch sent the speedy Carlos Gomez to pinch run. Before his first pitch to the next batter, Davis fired a snap throw over to first. Hosmer made a spectacular play to simultaneously field the short hop and tag the runner. Umpire Mike Everitt called Gomez safe. The Royals challenged the ruling. After a video review, the umpires called the runner out. Davis retired Altuve on a groundout to Moustakas to preserve the one-run victory.

Twelve outs away from falling into an 0-2 abyss, the Royals responded like cool battle-tested veterans. Their hitters delivered quality at-bats to put the ball in play. Cueto recovered from a rough start, and the bullpen dominated yet again with three scoreless innings. "It was a big come-from-behind victory and championship teams win those kind of games right there," Hosmer said.

Despite the triumph, the Royals knew they still faced a dangerous opponent. "Momentum can turn in a heartbeat," Cain said. The Boys in Blue now had to go to Houston, where they needed to take at least one game at Minute Maid Park to survive. "It's going to be a good series," Hinch said. "These are two really good teams."

ALDS GAME 3

With the series tied, Yost turned to his most consistent regular season starter. Edinson Volquez finished his first campaign in Kansas City with a 13-9 record and a 3.55 ERA. His 200 1/3 innings pitched led the staff. Signed to replace departing James Shields, the right hander delivered production that nearly equaled the numbers of his predecessor. But Volquez now had to face his toughest challenge to date as a Royal.

On the other side, Hinch deployed his most powerful weapon—Dallas Keuchel. The lefthander had dominated in the regular season, leading the league with 20 wins and 232 innings pitched. Even more daunting, the soon-to-be-named Cy Young winner posted a perfect 15-0 mark at home. The Royals had faced Keuchel twice during the regular season. They beat him at Kauffman in July, but he shut them down on June 30th with eight scoreless innings at Minute Maid Park—the site of this contest.

More than 42,000 fans filled the Houston stadium. They roared for the home team, while pounding together inflatable orange thundersticks. Some rooters sported fake beards as a tribute to Keuchel. Like Kansas Citians a year earlier, Astros fans had waited a long time to witness postseason baseball at their home park. After 91-year-old former president George

H.W. Bush threw out the ceremonial first pitch, the game was set to begin.

Leading off, Escobar reached base with an infield single. The Royals looked to follow the blueprint from their July victory over Keuchel by striking early and often. Instead, the Houston ace retired the next three batters. Volquez answered with a one-two-three effort in the bottom of the first. This pattern continued with neither team mounting a scoring threat in the first three innings.

Cain started the top of the fourth by crushing a hanging slider that cleared the façade above the left field seats. It was the KC centerfielder's first postseason home run. A subsequent error and a walk gave Kansas City two on with two out. Unfazed, Keuchel retired Gordon on a fly out to end the threat.

Volquez, meanwhile, continued to cruise. But after starting the bottom of the fifth by striking out Carlos Gomez, he walked Luis Valbuena. First baseman Chris Carter then rocketed a double into the left field corner, giving the Astros runners at second and third. Batting next, Jason Castro did not miss this RBI opportunity. The Houston catcher sent a grounder up the middle to drive in both runners and put his team in the lead.

An inning later, trouble brewed again when a warning track drive from George Springer barely eluded a lunging Cain for a double. After a groundout, an intentional walk to Rasmus gave the Astros runners at the corners. Volquez struck out Evan Gattis, but Gomez followed with an RBI-single to extend Houston's lead to 3-1.

Though they had put a man on base in five of the first six innings, the Royals could not capitalize on their scoring opportunities. Rios walked and advanced to third with two outs in the seventh, but Keuchel again escaped by striking out Cain. In the bottom of the inning, Carter homered off reliever Danny Duffy to add an insurance run for Houston. The Astros threatened to again pad their lead in the eighth after Carlos Correa singled and Rasmus launched a towering fly that struck a roof beam and dropped into shallow right for a hit. Royals reliever Luke Hochevar defused the crisis by retiring the next three batters.

Kansas City entered its last at-bat still trailing 4-1. Hinch called upon Gregerson to close things out. Alex Gordon kept his team's hopes alive by drilling an opposite-field homer to cut the lead to two. After Rios flew out to deep center, Escobar singled to bring the tying run to the plate. But Zobrist grounded into a fielder's choice and Cain went down swinging to end the game.

Now leading the ALDS two games to one, the upstart Astros had pushed the defending American League champions to the brink of elimination. Though not his sharpest outing, Keuchel continually battled out of trouble to deliver seven effective innings. He remained unbeaten at Minute Maid Park.

The Royals now had to win two consecutive games or their quest that began with such determination the previous winter would be over. "We have to stay confident," Cain said. Hosmer agreed. "We have to come back and do everything we can to win and take it back to Kansas City," the first baseman said.

ALDS GAME 4

On Monday, October 12th, the Royals arrived at the ballpark facing the possibility that their season could end this day—the first time all year the Damocles Sword of elimination dangled above them. To keep the thread from snapping, Yost called upon Yordano Ventura. The 24-year-old fireballer looked to improve on his two-inning outing in Game 1.

To finish off the series, Hinch gave the ball to 22-year-old rookie Lance McCullers. The right-hander had won only six games during the regular season, but posted a stingy 3.22 ERA and averaged more than a strikeout per inning. In his one start against Kansas City, McCullers had limited the Royals to just one run over seven innings. Hinch remained confident his young hurler had the tools to deliver a big performance, as long as he kept his emotions in check. "I have a lot of trust and faith that his stuff is as good as anybody we have and he'll be able to execute that," the Houston manager said, "provided that he can control the little animal inside him."

After neither team scored in the first inning, Moustakas walked with one out in the second. Perez followed by driving a McCullers fastball over the wall in right center. The opposite-field blast gave Kansas City an early 2-0 lead. In the bottom of the frame, however, Gomez drove a hanging breaking ball into the left field seats. An inning later, shortstop Carlos Correa belted a round-tripper to tie the game.

The contest remained deadlocked into the bottom of the fifth. After retiring the first two batters, Ventura courted trouble by walking Springer. Correa then delivered another big hit, shooting an RBI double down the right field line. Now pitching with the lead, McCullers sent Kansas City down in order in the top of the sixth.

With one out in the seventh, the Royals put a man on base when McCullers drilled Perez. Hoping to squash this rally before it got started, Hinch brought in Will Harris and his smothering 1.90 ERA. Yost sent speed-demon Terrance Gore to run for Perez. Gore wasted no time making this move look good. On the first pitch to Alex Gordon, he stole second to move into scoring position. But the KC left fielder went down swinging for the second out. With Rios batting, Gore sought to make something happen. He broke for third, easily stealing the base. But video replay overturned the call, marking the first failed steal attempt of Gore's major league career.

At the seventh-inning stretch, the Royals faced a daunting challenge. They had just six outs left in their season, and they had mustered only a single hit since the second inning. Though the deficit remained at one, stomachs across Royals Nation knotted and churned. And then, catastrophe struck. Correa and Rasmus homered off Madson in the bottom of the seventh, burying Kansas City in a four-run hole.

The string holding the sword above the Royals' heads snapped. The defending AL champions were about to fall to a team that had lost 111 games just two years earlier. Texas governor Greg Abbott posted a Tweet congratulating the Astros on their advance to the ALCS. Sportswriters for *The Kansas City Star* prepared to file their obituaries for the Royals. Columnist Sam Mellinger readied this assessment: "Best season in 35 years for Royals won't be remembered for a damn after this meltdown in Houston." Vahe Gregorian speculated that focusing on the postseason too soon disrupted the team's chemistry.

Though the game was not officially over, these stories might as well have gone to press. Baseball teams do not come back from four-run deficits in the eighth inning of a postseason game. The same team certainly can't do it in back-to-back years. If this were a movie script, a Royals comeback at this point would strain the limits of believability.

"Truth is stranger than fiction," Missourian Mark Twain once wrote, "but it is because Fiction is obliged to stick to possibilities; Truth isn't."

Top of the eighth. Rios singled. Escobar singled. Zobrist singled. Cain singled. Hosmer singled. Five straight hits to keep the line moving. Kansas City narrowed the deficit to two and loaded the bases with nobody out. Then came Morales's bouncer to Carlos Correa. The shortstop had destroyed the Royals with his bat; now he would use his leather to extinguish their late rally.

But after glancing off the pitcher's glove the ball had a tricky spin. It bounced higher than Correa expected. The sphere snuck past his glove and bounded into centerfield. Two Royals crossed the plate, tying the game. Hosmer stood at third and Morales at first. Still nobody out. The error sucked the life out of the stadium. Yost sent Jarrod Dyson to run for the lumbering Morales. The speedy outfielder stole second, but Moustakas struck out. Hinch brought in Luke Gregerson to try to stave off disaster. The right-hander walked Kansas City's backup catcher Drew Butera, a .196 hitter. Once again the Royals had the bases loaded.

Alex Gordon stepped to the plate. He needed just a fly ball to give his team the lead. He failed to do that, but delivered something just as good: a grounder to second that plated Hosmer. The fifth run of the inning gave the Royals a 7-6 lead. The crowd at Minute Maid Park watched in stunned silence.

Now in the driver's seat, Yost sent Wade Davis to pitch the bottom of the eighth. Dazed by a blue avalanche of runs, the Astros had no chance against The Terminator. Davis retired the side in order. In the top of the ninth, Hosmer launched a two-run homer into the Houston bullpen to extend the KC lead to 9-6. Davis allowed a leadoff single in the bottom of the ninth, before mowing down the next three Astros to close out the game.

Much like they had done a year earlier in the Wild Card game, the Royals escaped elimination with an improbable late-inning comeback. How in the name of Dane Iorg did that happen? "Obviously, we're pretty late in the game right there and down by four, so not one guy can get us back in this game," Hosmer said. "So we got to do whatever we can to keep the line moving." Gordon credited Moose's eighth-inning tirade with firing up the team to do what needed to be done. Moustakas noted that his exact words at that moment could not be printed. "This is what we do," Moose said in calmer postgame circumstances, "never quit and never give up." Cain concurred. "I wouldn't say it's easy," the centerfielder said, "but we found a way in the wild-card game last year and we found a way today in a big win-or-go-home situation here."

The ALDS was tied at two games apiece. The deciding Game 5 would be played at Kauffman Stadium in Kansas City. Though battered with a devastating setback, the Astros were determined to show up strong and make the outcome of Game 4 moot. Carlos Correa told reporters that his team was not out of it. "We have to go out and try to win the next game," the shortstop said, "and everybody will forget about this game."

ALDS GAME 5

Questions abounded before the fifth and deciding contest of the American League Division Series. Game 1 winner Collin

McHugh would start for Houston, but would manager A.J. Hinch call upon ace Dallas Keuchel at some point in the evening? In a similar situation a year earlier, the Giants used Madison Bumgarner in relief to subdue the Royals in Game 7 of the World Series. The other big question for the Astros was how would their 21-year-old shortstop rebound from a major miscue? In Game 4, before his eighth-inning error, Carlos Correa had ripped four hits with four RBIs. Could he put the past behind him and deliver again? Could his teammates?

With Johnny Cueto starting Game 5, the Royals similarly faced big questions. After struggling with declining velocity the final two months of the regular season and allowing four earned runs in Game 2, the so-called ace had done little to instill confidence in his new employers. Yost would give Cueto the ball, but he had a short leash. "If we're not comfortable with his stuff and he's not getting outs, he's coming out of the game," pitching coach Dave Eiland said. *Kansas City Star* columnist Vahe Gregorian summarized the angst of Royals Nation when he wrote, "We have no idea what we are getting [tonight]."

Prior to the game, the Royals paid tribute to Larry Leggio and John Mesh, two Kansas City firefighters who died two days earlier battling a blaze at an apartment building. Royals players had worn Kansas City Fire Department hats and shirts for their off-day batting practice. During the pregame ceremony, the Kauffman crowd cheered the families of the firemen, as well as the other members of the KC fire department, who lined up along the first-base line. A moment of silence followed. Several Royals hugged the firefighters and family members as they exited the field after the ceremony.

Despite all the questions about him, Cueto woke up on the day of Game 5 feeling confident. His team's comeback in the previous contest had inspired him. Knowing that Kansas City had acquired him for games like this, he prepared to show up big at The K. He told Escobar before the game that he would pitch more than seven innings. His shortstop replied, "I know, I trust you man."

Cueto provided hope that his prediction was on the mark by sending the Astros down in order in the top of the first. The good feelings, however, dissipated in the second inning. With two outs, Gattis reached base on an infield hit when Moustakas's long throw pulled Hosmer off the bag. Luis Valbuena then blasted a homer into the Royals bullpen in right field. Murmurs of unease rippled throughout the ballpark. Kansas City's top ace had once again placed his team in an early hole. And this time if the Royals could not come back, their season was over.

In the bottom of the fourth, Cain singled on a check swing flare that fell into right field. Hosmer then worked the count full. On the payoff pitch, Cain took off. Hoz dropped a single into center. When Astros outfielder Carlos Gomez slipped trying to field the ball, Cain continued running and scored without a throw. The Royals had cut the deficit in half.

Cueto retired Houston in order in the top of the fifth. Pitch magnet Salvador Perez led off Kansas City's half of the frame by getting hit by an errant curveball. The tying run had reached base. Gordon followed by launching a McHugh cutter to deep right. The ball bounced on the warning track and bounded over the fence for a ground-rule double that put runners at second and third. Hinch summoned Mike Fiers to relieve McHugh. Rios welcomed the new pitcher by bouncing a double down the left field line. Both runners scored, giving Kansas City the lead. After Escobar bunted to advance Rios to third, Zobrist lofted a fly to right center. The ball carried deep enough for Rios to tag up and score. The Royals led 4-2. Blue-clad fans roared their approval.

As the dark clouds of elimination gathered above them, the Astros struggled in vain to solve Cueto. The dreadlocked one sent them down in order in the sixth. And the seventh. And the eighth. No Houston batter had reached base since Valbuena's home run in the second inning. Providing an emphatic answer to his doubters, Cueto retired 19 straight batters.

With his team down to its final three outs, Hinch brought in Keuchel to pitch the eighth. To have any chance at a comeback,

Houston could not afford to fall behind any further. But Escobar greeted the soon-to-be-named Cy Young winner by shooting a double down the right field line. Following a Zobrist line out, Keuchel intentionally walked Cain. One out later, Morales crushed a curveball into the seats in left center for a three-run homer. Game, set, and match.

In a mere formality, Davis sent the Astros down in order in the ninth. After right fielder Paulo Orlando corralled the final out, a barrage of fireworks exploded above the ballpark. "Kansas City/Hey, Hey, Hey" blared from the Kauffman Stadium speakers. The players bounced about in a celebratory scrum on the infield. Rallying from the brink of elimination, the Boys in Blue would advance.

Dayton Moore's big midseason trade now looked better than ever. "Johnny Cueto was unbelievable," Yost said. His Astros counterpart agreed. "The good version of Johnny Cueto is really tough," Hinch said. Kansas City's other major trade acquisition praised his fellow newcomer. "He [Cueto] is that guy that they thought he was in that trade and he came through in the biggest way we needed him tonight," Zobrist said.

Not since Don Larsen's perfect game in the 1956 World Series had an American League pitcher retired the final 19 batters he faced in a postseason game. Cueto had delivered on his pregame prediction. After the victory he reiterated, "Today was the game that I was going to show everybody what I'm all about in big games."

Champagne flowed and sprayed throughout the Royals clubhouse. Jeremy Guthrie led the raucous postgame celebration. With his goggled teammates gathered around, the veteran pitcher yelled, "I need two claps and a Ric Flair for John Cueto!" After the subsequent Nature Boy "Wooooo!" Guthrie yelled, "I need two claps and a Ric Flair for Morales!" And so the revelry continued.

The ALDS hurdle had been cleared. It had not been easy. And the next barrier loomed even more perilous.

Chapter 11

A.L. Championship Series

The Toronto Blue Jays awaited Kansas City in the next round of the playoffs. This was the American League Championship Series matchup baseball fans had been anticipating since mid-August. But, similar to the Royals, the Blue Jays almost fell in the ALDS to an upstart team from Texas. After losing their first two games at home to the Rangers, Toronto stormed back to take the next three. In the deciding game, Texas led by a run just nine outs from advancing. But the Rangers committed three errors in the bottom of the seventh. Blue Jays slugger Jose Bautista provided the decisive blow with a three-run homer, followed by an emphatic bat flip.

And so the Boys in Blue would face their most formidable pennant obstacle to date. Like the Royals a year earlier, Toronto entered the season riding the longest playoff drought in baseball. Not since 1993 had the team played meaningful games in October. The Blue Jays ended that dismal run by catching fire in the season's second half. Toronto went 40-18 after July, winning 11 in a row at one point. The team sizzled in August to take control of the AL East. By vanquishing the Rangers in the divisional series, Toronto set up a rematch of the 1985 ALCS won by Dick Howser's Royals.

An offensive juggernaut, Toronto led the majors in home runs (232), slugging average (.457), OPS (.797) and runs per game (5.5). This Canadian Murderer's Row featured three sluggers with at least 39 home runs: Josh Donaldson, Jose Bautista, and Edwin Encarnacion. The team's fourth leading home run hitter, catcher Russell Martin, had knocked 23 out of the park. No Royal hit more than 22 homers. And the Blue Jays could run, with just 16 fewer steals than the Royals during the regular season.

While Kansas City held a slight edge in team earned run average, the Royals starters' 4.34 regular season ERA was the worst among the 10 playoff teams. Toronto, on the other hand, could deploy two former Cy Young winners: R.A. Dickey and David Price. A mid-season acquisition from Detroit, Price went 9-1 after arriving in Canada at the end of July. Starters Marcus Stroman and Marco Estrada combined for a 6-0 mark in September, giving the Blue Jays two more rotation weapons. Toronto boasted strong bullpen arms too with Roberto Osuna and Aaron Sanchez, but an ALDS injury to Brett Cecil took away an important lefty option.

The Royals entered the series with a few advantages of their own. Kansas City batters struck out with less frequency than any other MLB team, creating a nice matchup with the Toronto pitchers' sixth-lowest K-rate. And with its stable of far-ranging Gold Glove-caliber fielders, Kansas City led the AL with 56 defensive runs saved—easily besting Toronto's 15 DRS. The Royals still had a fearsome bullpen too. But aside from Wade Davis and Luke Hochevar, the KC relievers showed some vulnerability in the ALDS. Astro batters torched Ryan Madson, and scored against Herrera and Duffy. With Greg Holland out for the season, how much of an advantage would Kansas City's bullpen provide?

The Blue Jays had bested the Royals four out of seven times during the regular season. In their final meeting, both benches cleared during an ugly game that featured three hit batters, several brushback pitches, three ejections, and a slew of combative bulletin board quotes. Edinson Volquez called Josh Donaldson "a little baby." Jose Bautista tweeted that he had lost respect for Ned Yost. Fans and commentators wondered if the bad blood from that August encounter would carry over into the playoffs.

Despite Kansas City's better record (by two games) and home field advantage, a majority of national baseball pundits viewed Toronto as the American League's best team. Their lineup appeared ready to feast upon the Royals' suspect starting pitching. Citing the Blue Jays' offensive firepower and improved second-half rotation, Grantland's Ben Lindbergh predicted that Toronto would prevail in six. The leading Vegas sportsbooks agreed, favoring the Blue Jays to take the ALCS.

With their determined quest to return to the World Series, the Royals had a great run in 2015. But Kansas City just had the misfortune of running into Canada's version of the 1927 Yankees. Hopefully the Boys in Blue would at least put up a fight.

ALCS GAME 1

Ned Yost entrusted the hill to Edinson Volquez for the opening game of the AL championship series. Having absorbed one of his team's two losses in the previous round, the right-hander looked to rebound with a strong outing. That he was facing Toronto further increased his incentive. As the starting pitcher when the two teams last met, Volquez helped light some of the fireworks. After Josh Donaldson registered his disapproval of being pitched inside, Volquez said he "was crying like a baby." The slugging third baseman countered by describing Volquez as "some pretty good hitting."

Toronto manager John Gibbons gave the ball to Marco Estrada. Relying on vertically-moving fastballs and change-ups, the right-hander often induced routine fly balls and weakly-hit grounders. After a slow start to the season, Estrada heated up in the summer to finish at 13-8 with a 3.13 ERA. Along the way, he allowed an American League-low .203 batting average to opposing hitters. Gibbons credited him with helping to save Toronto's season.

Prior to the game, Volquez planned to pitch the Blue Jays inside again, just as he had done in August. Reviewing the power-hitting pull hitters that comprised the Toronto lineup, Salvador Perez offered an alternate strategy. "How you feel pitching down and away?" the catcher asked his starter. Volquez replied, "I feel sexy throwing down and away." So the Kansas City battery changed the game plan.

Perez's idea looked like the right call early on. Volquez allowed only two Blue Jays to reach base—both on walks—over the first three innings. Estrada started strong as well, until Alex Gordon led off the bottom of the third by smoking a double into the right field corner. After Alex Rios struck out, Alcides Escobar shot a grounder down the right field line for an RBI double. One out later, Lorenzo Cain drilled a hit through the right side to plate Escobar. Kansas City led 2-0. An inning later, Perez deposited an Estrada fastball over the left field wall to extend the lead to three.

Volquez continued dealing. He allowed the first Blue Jay hit in the fourth, but still turned in another shutout frame. The Toronto fifth similarly passed with one hit and no runs. In the sixth inning, however, Volquez flirted with disaster. He started the frame by walking his nemesis, Josh Donaldson. The pitcher then walked Jose Bautista to put two men on for the dangerous Edwin Encarnacion. The DH had slugged .557 with 111 RBIs during the regular season. After a mound visit from Dave Eiland, Volquez struck him out looking with a 95-mph fastball on the outside corner. Next batted first baseman Chris Colabello, a .321 hitter with power. He drilled a fastball hard to left, but Gordon was there to snare the drive. Toronto's last chance to capitalize on the walks came with shortstop Troy Tulowitzki, a five-time All-Star acquired from Colorado just before the trading deadline. With the towel-waving Kauffman crowd on its feet, Volquez struck him out looking.

Happy with six shutout innings from his starter, Ned Yost turned to his bullpen for the seventh. Pitching in his customary role, Kelvin Herrera sent the Blue Jays down in order. Taking over for the eighth, Ryan Madson courted trouble. After allowing a one-out single to Donaldson, he walked Bautista. Toronto again had the tying run at the plate. But with Encarnacion out of the game due to a strained finger ligament, Gibbons sent lefty slugger Justin Smoak to the plate. Madson retired him on a pop foul to Hosmer. Colabello bounced out to second to end the threat.

In the bottom of the eighth, the Royals put two on with one out. Not letting this opportunity go to waste, Eric Hosmer smashed a drive off the right field wall for an RBI double. Morales plated another run with a sac fly. The insurance runs convinced Yost to give Wade Davis another day of rest. The manager sent Luke Hochevar to pitch the ninth. Though one batter reached on an error, the Blue Jays again went down without scoring. Kansas City completed a 5-0 victory.

Royals pitchers had shut down the vaunted Toronto lineup with just three hits. In addition to feeling sexy, Volquez said he benefitted from an abundance of energy. With this extra juice, his fastball velocity increased to the mid-90s, his highest speed since 2012. "I was just making my pitches," he said. His performance even earned praise from the opposing manager. "His ball was ducking and darting everywhere," said Gibbons, a former Royals bench coach.

After his team needed three come-from-behind wins to get past the Astros, Eric Hosmer appreciated the change of pace. "There's only so many crazy comebacks you can pull off in a postseason," the first baseman said. "It was nice to get out to a lead tonight."

ALCS GAME 2

For the second game, Kansas City would have to face arguably the best starting pitcher on either roster. Over the past seven seasons David Price had reigned as one of the top hurlers in the American League. In 2012 the lefthander won 20 games for Tampa Bay, capturing the Cy Young Award. The five-time All-Star teamed with former Royal James Shields to form an effective one-two punch for the Rays for several years. Price began the 2015 season with Detroit. When the Tigers fell out of contention, they traded him to Toronto. Continuing his mound prowess, Price posted a season mark of 18-5 with an AL best 2.45 ERA. The southpaw had faced Kansas City twice during the regular season—both times as a Tiger. In his first outing, he allowed just one run in a complete-game win. A week later, Price gave up 13 hits in 6 1/3 innings, taking a no decision in the Tigers ninth-inning walk-off victory.

Yordano Ventura would toe the rubber for the Royals. The 24-year-old was not particularly effective in either of his ALDS starts, posting a 7.71 ERA against the Astros. The young fireballer looked to turn things around against Toronto. Ventura beat the Blue Jays in his only start against them in the regular season.

After Kansas City native and golf legend Tom Watson threw out the ceremonial first pitch, the Royals took the field. Both starters looked strong early on. In the top of the third, however, Blue Jays centerfielder Kevin Pillar sliced a leadoff double into right. Second baseman Ryan Goins followed by shooting a double down the left field line to plate Pillar.

Aside from that hiccup Ventura remained sharp, sending the Blue Jays down without a run in the fourth and the fifth. Unfortunately for the home team, Price confounded the Royals with his cutters, heaters, and change-ups. After allowing Escobar to lead off the game with a single, he retired the next 15 Royals batters to carry a one-hit shutout through five innings. In the top of the sixth, Donaldson chopped an infield single and Bautista followed with a walk. Back in the lineup, Encarnacion smacked a sharp grounder into left to drive in Donaldson. Ventura rebounded to strike out Colabello, but then gave up a Tulowitzski double that scored another run. Toronto led 3-0.

And the way Price was dealing, the lead looked insurmountable. The lefty ace retired the Royals in order again in the sixth to push his streak to 18 straight batters.

In the bottom of the seventh, Ben Zobrist lofted a pop fly into shallow right. He slammed his bat to the ground in disgust. When the ball was caught, the Royals would be down to their final eight outs in the game. But with the crowd roaring, Toronto's right fielder Bautista and second baseman Goins each thought the other was going to catch it. The ball dropped in for a single. And that was all it took to open the floodgates.

Cain lined an opposite-field single into right. Hosmer followed with a hit into left center that plated Zobrist. Morales rolled a grounder to shortstop that scored Cain. Moustakas then drilled a hit into right, driving in Hosmer. One out later, Gordon laced a double into right center, scoring Moose. After Gibbons called in Aaron Sanchez to relieve the shell-shocked Price, Rios grounded a hit up the middle to drive in Gordon. An inning that had started with a harmless pop up to right, snowballed into an avalanche of Royals runs. Held in check for six innings, Kansas City now led 5-3.

After Herrera tossed a scoreless eighth, Moose delivered an RBI single to increase the KC lead to three. But baseball's most prolific offense was not finished. Pillar started the ninth with a single off Wade Davis. Pinch hitter Cliff Pennington followed with a walk, bringing the tying run to the plate. And then The Terminator activated. Davis struck out the next two batters, and retired Bautista on a fly out to end the game.

The underdog Royals now led the ALCS two games to none. And once again, Kansas City had rallied from a multiple-run deficit to win a postseason game. "Our guys never quit," Yost said. "They keep going." With the way Price was pitching, it appeared the game was headed for a Toronto victory. But the Boys in Blue broke through. "We just needed to find a way to get a runner on base so we could do what we can," Moustakas said, "keep the line moving."

The Royals bullpen again proved invaluable by holding the opposition in check with the game on the line. Especially crucial was the contribution of Luke Hochevar, who entered the game in the sixth with the bases loaded and just one out. With the Blue Jays threatening to break things open, the reliever retired the next two hitters to keep Kansas City in the game. Duffy, Herrera, and Davis followed with three scoreless innings. "You know when you have a lead and hand it off to those guys," Hosmer said, "you have a lot of confidence."

On the other side, Price fell to 0-7 in postseason starts. He and his teammates would have to try to regroup after a disastrous collapse. They had the advantage of returning to Toronto for the next three games. And they had the recent memory of falling behind 0-2 in the ALDS, before storming back to win three straight elimination games. As Jose Bautista said, "We still have more of a chance to come out victorious in this series than we did in the last series."

ALCS GAME 3

Facing a must-win game, John Gibbons turned to 24-year-old Marcus Stroman. Shelved for most of the season due to a torn ACL in his left knee, the right-hander returned to win all four of his September starts with a 1.67 ERA. He also pitched the decisive Game 5 in the ALDS, limiting the Rangers to two runs over six innings. An imposing mound presence, the young starter prevented hard contact with deceptively-moving sliders and curves.

Kansas City similarly called upon its ALDS Game 5 starter. Johnny Cueto hoped for a repeat of his brilliant outing that propelled his team into this round. The right-hander had made one regular season start against the Blue Jays in 2015, allowing three runs over six innings. He left the game with the lead, but the Royals bullpen faltered and Toronto prevailed in eleven.

Nearly 50,000 boisterous fans packed the Rogers Centre for the first ALCS game in Toronto since 1993. The Blue Jays looked to regain their power stroke at the hitter-friendly ballpark known as the homer dome. Leading off the game, Alcides Escobar drilled a liner into right that got past Bautista for a triple. Esky then scored when Zobrist grounded to second. But Kansas City's early lead did not quiet the rowdy crowd. When Cueto took the hill in the bottom of the first, fans taunted him with a sing-song chant of "Cueee-to, Cueee-to." Such serenading dated back to October 2013, when Cueto pitched for the Reds in the NL Wild Card game at Pittsburgh. With Pirates fans chanting his name, Cueto allowed eight hits in 3 1/3 innings and took the loss. Two years later, Blue Jays fans similarly tried to get inside the head of the dreadlocked one.

Early on, it appeared the crowd noise would have no effect. Cueto allowed a walk but no runs in the first. The second inning, however, was a different story. After Tulowitzki delivered a one-out single, Cueto plunked Russell Martin's elbow guard. Kevin Pillar grounded into a force that put runners on the corners. The Jays centerfielder stole second to move into scoring position. Goins then slapped a single to left, driving home both runners. Following a walk to left fielder Ben Revere, Donaldson grounded a single through the left side, plating Goins. Toronto led 3-1.

Kansas City struck back in its next at-bat. With one out in the third, Zobrist belted a Stroman cutter off the base of the wall in center for a double. Cain sent a grounder up the middle that found Tulowitzki's glove, but the shortstop could not make a throw. The infield single gave Cain a 12-game postseason hitting streak, a new franchise record. Hosmer drove home Zobrist with a chopper to first, and the Royals had narrowed the gap to one.

Encarnacion led off the bottom of the third with a single. Colabello followed by drawing a four-pitch walk. Cueto then served a tasty fastball up in the zone to Tulowitzki, who deposited it over the centerfield wall. Toronto led 6-2. And the Canadians were not finished. Cueto walked Martin and gave up an RBI double to Pillar. Yost brought in Kris Medlen to try to stop the bleeding. The move appeared to work when the reliever retired the next two batters. But Donaldson crushed a breaking ball into the second deck in left to drive home two more runs. Leading 9-2 after three innings, the Blue Jays had put this one out of reach.

But the Royals didn't get the memo that this game was over. In the fifth, Escobar singled and Zobrist doubled to put runners at second and third. With Hosmer at the plate, a wild pitch scored Escobar and sent Zobrist to third. Two batters later, Moustakas ripped as single to plate another run. Kansas City had cut the lead to 9-4.

In the bottom of the fifth, Goins hammered a solo shot off Medlen. Three innings later, Bautista tagged Franklin Morales with an RBI single to push the Toronto lead back to seven. Though they had just three outs left, Yost's boys still refused to give up. Escobar led off the ninth with an infield hit. Zobrist followed with his third double of the game. A sacrifice fly from Cain and a Hosmer single plated both runners. This uprising concerned Gibbons enough for him to summon his closer, Roberto Osuna. Morales greeted the reliever by smashing a Titanic blast into the second deck in right. The two-run shot cut the once insurmountable Toronto lead to 11-8. But Osuna recovered to retire Moustakas and Perez on groundouts to end the game.

Toronto garnered a win it had to have, but Kansas City's four-run outburst in the ninth showed that no lead was safe against the Boys in Blue. "We're just going to keep fighting," said Alex Gordon. "We've got a lot of competitors on this team, and that's what you see." Hosmer similarly saw a silver lining after the game. "We're still up in the series 2-1," the first baseman said, "and the way we're swinging the bats on offense, we like where we're at."

Despite this optimism, the defeat ended a nine-game ALCS winning streak for the Royals. Heading into Game 3 with a chance to deliver a crushing blow that would all but secure the pennant, Kansas City now faced the prospect of Toronto tying the series the next day.

ALCS GAME 4

Yost gave the ball to Chris Young for the fourth game. Originally slated as a long reliever, the tall 36-year-old came through big during a season in which the Royals rotation was racked with injuries and ineffectiveness. Making 18 starts, Young finished the regular season with an 11-6 record and a 3.06 ERA. But he lost his only start against the Blue Jays. To make matters worse, Young was a fly ball pitcher—a potentially disastrous liability in the homer dome.

Similar to Yost, Gibbons would entrust the mound to a seasoned veteran for Game 4. In 2015 R.A. Dickey turned in his fifth-straight 200-inning season. A Cy Young winner in 2012, the right-hander relied on a baffling knuckleball to remain effective at age 40. Like his team, Dickey got hot in the second half, going 8-1 after the All-Star break. He shut down the Royals on August 2nd, allowing no runs and just two hits over seven innings.

The opposing hurlers starting this game had been teammates twice during their careers—with the Rangers more than a decade ago and with the Mets more recently. Only once before in ALCS history had the combined ages of the starters exceeded that of Dickey (40) and Young (36). And one of these old men was about to have a bad day.

Escobar led off the game by dropping a bunt single down the third base line. In so doing, he became the first player in MLB history to lead off four straight games of a postseason series with a hit. Zobrist followed by clobbering a high knuckleball over the right field wall. After drawing a walk, Cain stole second. Hosmer then singled to put runners at the corners. With Morales at the plate, catcher Russell Martin let a knuckleball slip by for a passed ball. Cain raced home and slid under Dickey's tag to score. Hosmer advanced to third on a bouncer to the right side and then came home on a sacrifice fly by Moustakas. Kansas City led 4-0.

Young allowed a walk in the bottom of the first, but struck out three Blue Jays to squash any scoring chances. Royals hitters went to work again in the second. After a Gordon ground out, Alex Rios blasted a fat knuckleball over the wall in left center. Dickey then hit Escobar on the hand. One out later, he walked Cain. Gibbons had seen enough. He brought in Liam Hendricks to put out the fire for his beleaguered starter.

Though trailing 5-0, Toronto did not give up. With one out in the bottom of the third, Ryan Goins dropped a flare into left center. Young then walked Ben Revere to put two men on for the dangerous Josh Donaldson. The self-proclaimed "Bringer of Rain" ripped a slider into the left field corner. The ball hopped up off the turf and skipped over the wall for a ground-rule double. One run scored and the Blue Jays had runners at second and third. Bautista followed with a chopper that plated Revere, cutting the Kansas City lead to 5-2.

Young retired the next six batters he faced, but with two outs in the fifth, he gave up a single to Revere. With just a three-run lead, Yost did not want to take any chances against Donaldson. The skipper summoned Hochevar, who retired the rain-bringer on a foul pop to Hosmer.

The score remained 5-2 until the top of the seventh, when Kansas City loaded the bases with a Perez walk and back-to-back singles from Gordon and Rios. A deep sacrifice fly from Escobar and a wild pitch scored two runs for the Royals. Following a Zobrist walk, Cain delivered an RBI-single and Hosmer hit a sac fly to plate KC's eighth and ninth runs.

Though the fat lady had started warming up her vocal cords, the Royals offense wasn't finished with its assault on Toronto's hapless bullpen. In the top of the eighth, Escobar drove in Perez with a sacrifice fly. Cain later drilled a single up the middle that brought home two more tallies. Having depleted his bullpen, Gibbons sent infielder Cliff Pennington to pitch the ninth. Kansas City plated two more runs. The final score of this public flogging was 14-2.

"Hitting is contagious, and baseball is about momentum," Gordon said after the Royals' scoring outburst, a postseason franchise record. The winds of momentum had shifted with gale-force strength back to the team from Missouri. Former Blue Jay Alex Rios led the way by going three for three with a homer, as the fans who once cheered him showered him with boos. Four other Royals rapped multiple hits. "We like the way we're playing right now," Yost said. "Our offense has been really, really good."

Just eight days removed from a harrowing near-elimination experience in Houston, the Royals arrived at the brink of their second consecutive pennant. Chris Young recognized the distinctive qualities of his team. "There's a comfort level these guys have, where they know this is something special," the pitcher said. "I don't know how to explain it, but it really is tremendous."

ALCS GAME 5

The Royals rolled into the Rogers Centre for Game 5 with all the advantages. Only 12 of the 79 major league teams that had led a best-of-seven postseason series three games to one had failed to win the series. Kansas City, moreover, had outscored Toronto 33-16 in the four ALCS games thus far. And the pitching matchup would be a rematch of Game 1 with Edinson Volquez squaring off against Marco Estrada. Volquez had dominated the Blue Jays in that contest, allowing just two hits over six shutout innings.

With nearly 50,000 screaming Blue Jays fans hoping they were not watching their team for the last time this season, Estrada retired the Royals three-up, three-down in the first. Volquez matched him. Estrada again retired the side in order in the second. In the bottom half of the frame, Colabello unloaded on a hanging Volquez change-up, sending it deep over the wall in center. The game then settled into a pitchers' duel.

Escobar recorded the first Kansas City hit in the fourth. But a double play and a pop out again kept the Royals from scoring. After singling in the bottom of the frame, Bautista was similarly erased by a twin-killing. The score remained 1-0 heading to the sixth. Estrada sent the Royals down in order. At this point, he had faced the minimum possible 18 batters.

The way his counterpart was dealing, Volquez needed to keep the game close for Kansas City to have a chance. Instead, the opposite happened. Revere led off the sixth with a walk. Volquez then hit Donaldson with an inside fastball. Though unintentional, the fans booed lustily. Now in a jam, Volquez walked Bautista on a full-count pitch that caught a lot of the strike zone. The missed call gave Toronto the bases loaded with nobody out. The frustrated KC starter then walked Encarnacion to force in a run. Yost brought in Kelvin Herrera to try to limit the damage. The fireballing reliever provided hope that disaster could be averted when he struck out Colabello. But Tulowitzki pounded a fastball deep to left center for a bases-clearing double. Toronto led 5-0. An inning later Donaldson and Bautista thumped back-to-back doubles off Danny Duffy to extend the lead to six.

Estrada, meanwhile, continued to plow through the Royals lineup. Finally, with two outs in the eighth, he made a mistake to Salvador Perez. The big catcher drilled an opposite-field home run to get his team on the board. When Gordon followed with a base hit, Gibbons called for Aaron Sanchez. Estrada left the field to a standing ovation. Rios singled off Sanchez, but Escobar flew out to end the threat.

Perez's dinger turned out to be the lone highlight in a dismal game for the Boys in Blue. Toronto pushed across another run in the eighth, and Osuna retired the Royals in order in the ninth to finish off the 7-1 victory.

With their backs to the wall, Toronto got a big game performance from Estrada. "This time around I had a better fastball command," the pitcher said. "That was the key to the game." His performance earned the respect of the Royals. "He threw the ball down, down and away, down and in," Alcides Escobar said. "He didn't miss many pitches today."

Estrada's masterpiece overshadowed a mostly solid outing from his counterpart. Moustakas said Volquez had a great day, but "he just had one inning get away from him and that happens." Hitting 98-mph with his fastball early on left Volquez low on gas later in the game. The starter then lost his rhythm coming to the plate.

Despite the setback, the Royals remained confident. With the series returning to Kauffman Stadium, they would have two chances to close out the pennant. As Yost told reporters, "we're taking a three game to two lead back to where we are comfortable and back to our home fans that support us and are fantastic." Gaining home field advantage at the end of the season had indeed proved significant.

ALCS GAME 6

After five games, a disturbing pattern had emerged in the ALCS. Disturbing from the Royals' point of view that is. In 1985 when these two teams met in the league championship series, Toronto won its first two games at home. Kansas City won Game 3 at Royals Stadium, but lost Game 4 to fall into a 3-1 hole. Facing elimination, Danny Jackson tossed a gem in Game 5 to keep the Royals alive. Kansas City then won the final two games at Toronto to capture the pennant. Thirty years later, the ALCS was following the exact same win-loss pattern, though with the teams reversed. If this trend continued, the Blue Jays would win Games 6 and 7 on the road to complete the comeback. While these were completely different teams playing now, the pattern troubled many in Royals Nation.

Even more distressing for Kansas City fans, their boys would again have to face David Price. The ace had shut down the Royal bats for six innings in his previous start, before a misplayed pop fly threw him off track. With a little better luck, could he steamroll the Boys in Blue for an entire game?

Yordano Ventura took the hill for the Royals. The right-hander was looking for his first win in the 2015 playoffs—a triumph that would send his team back to the World Series. The stakes were high. Ned Yost would likely keep his young starter on a short leash.

Trouble began for the Royals with the first batter of the game. Blue Jays leadoff hitter Ben Revere drilled a fastball down the right field line for a double. Was this an early sign that the reverse pattern of the 1985 ALCS was indeed in effect? Answering to the negative, Ventura retired Donaldson, Bautista, and Encarnacion to squelch the threat. In the bottom of the frame, Zobrist drove a cutter from his former Rays teammate into the left field seats to give Kansas City an early lead. An inning later, Moustakas stepped to the plate. After writing his mother Connie's initials in the dirt with the end of his bat, he belted a change-up just over the right field wall to increase the margin to 2-0.

Staked to an early lead, Ventura rolled through the Toronto lineup. After Revere's leadoff double, he sent down the next 10 Blue Jays in a row. But with one out in the fourth, Bautista rocketed a belt-high fastball a mile over the wall in left. With Kansas City's lead cut in half, tensions increased at The K.

This angst escalated in the fifth when Ventura walked the first two batters. After a visit from Dave Eiland, the pitcher recovered to retire the next three Blue Jays. An inning later, however, Encarnacion hammered a fastball into the gap in left center for a double. With the tying run in scoring position with just one out, Yost called in Herrera from the bullpen. Cranking up the heat to 100 mph, the flamethrower struck out Colabello and induced a fly out from Troy Tulowitzki to preserve the KC lead.

Price, meanwhile, pitched effectively to keep his team close. After he sent the Royals down in order in the sixth, the contest entered its final three innings with the score still 2-1. Moustakas led off the Kansas City seventh by dropping a broken-bat blooper into center. Following a Perez fly out, Gordon advanced the runner to second with a grounder to Goins. Seeking a righty-righty matchup, Gibbons brought in Sanchez to face Rios. The strategy backfired when the right fielder roped a hit into left field, scoring Moustakas. The much-needed insurance run pushed Kansas City's lead to 3-1.

As rain clouds gathered above, Yost sent Ryan Madson to pitch the eighth. After Revere led off the inning with an infield hit, many fans wondered why Wade Davis was not in the game. Just six outs from a pennant, why not call upon the most dominant closer in baseball? The answer was weather-related. Yost did not want to bring in Davis with rain on the way. If a lengthy delay ensued, he would then have to remove his most valuable bullpen weapon from the game. Remaining on the mound, Madson struck out Donaldson looking. Bautista then stepped to the plate. Cementing his status as one of the least popular Blue Jays in KC, the slugger smoked a high fastball into the left field seats. Suddenly the game was tied, dousing the celebratory atmosphere that had been building in the stadium. After Madson walked Encarnacion, Yost brought in Davis, who retired the next two batters to end the inning.

The rain arrived as expected. Umpires halted play and the Kauffman grounds crew covered the infield. During the delay anxious Royals fans stewed about their manager's blunder. Why didn't Davis start the eighth inning? Was the pennant slipping away? Were the Boys in Blue about to get Yosted?

After 45 minutes, play resumed. Gibbons sent Osuna to pitch the eighth. Leading off the inning, Cain drew a walk. Hosmer followed by ripping a drive into the right field corner. Bautista cut it off on one bounce to prevent an extra-base hit. Royals third base coach Mike Jirschele then made a bold decision that caught the Blue Jays off-guard. Aware from scouting reports of Bautista's habit of throwing to second base in such situations, Jirschele waved the runner home. As the ball flew toward second, Cain rounded third and raced toward the plate. Easily beating the throw, he slid home with the go-ahead score. The towel-waving crowd exploded. Kansas City was just three outs from a pennant.

Leading 4-3, Yost sent Davis back out to pitch the ninth. This was something of a gamble given that his closer had not thrown a pitch in over an hour. Would The Terminator be rusty? Davis insisted he was ready. Russell Martin led off the inning with a single. Gibbons replaced Martin with pinch runner Dalton Pompey, who promptly stole second. A few pitches later, the speedster swiped third. Toronto had the tying run ninety feet away with nobody out. Pillar walked, putting Blue Jays at the corners. Now in a tight spot, Davis struck out pinch hitter Dioner Navarro to record a crucial out. But on the third strike, Pillar stole second. A single could give Toronto the lead. After falling behind Revere 2-0, Davis rebounded to strike out the outfielder. That brought soon-to-be-named MVP Josh Donaldson to the plate for an Old West-style gunslinger shootout. Up in his box, a nervous George Brett checked his pulse. With the count 2-1, The Terminator fired. Donaldson swung. Instead of a run-scoring deluge, the Bringer of Rain brought a ground ball to third. Moustakas fielded it and fired over to Hosmer. "Royals win it!" exclaimed longtime Kansas City broadcaster Denny Matthews, after the pennant-clinching play.

Once again, fireworks exploded above the stadium. Once again the Royals formed a scrum on the Kauffman infield to celebrate a series victory. And once again, champagne sprays and Ric Flair *woooos* flew about the clubhouse. "Our guys, from the first day of spring training, their focus was to get back to the World Series," a jubilant Yost said, "and they did it." Late-inning hits again proved decisive. "We just try to put quality at-bats together," Gordon said. "No one is afraid of being up in that spot." Dayton Moore noted that this success was a long time coming. "The core group has grown up together in the minor leagues and they have wanted to do something special here in Kansas City for a long time," the GM said. "They are motivated, they are focused, they are determined to win."

A host of stellar performances had carried the Royals to victory over the powerful Blue Jays. Hosmer delivered six RBIs in the series. Moustakas and Cain drove in five apiece. Rios batted .368. Kelvin Herrera, Luke Hochevar, and Wade Davis combined for 11 1/3 scoreless innings out of the bullpen. And Alcides Escobar was named series MVP after batting .478 with six runs scored and five RBIs.

The Royals had thus proved that 2014 was not a fluke. The team claimed back-to-back pennants for the first time in franchise history. "The story just keeps getting better and better," said Hosmer. But could the Boys in Blue write a different ending this time?

Chapter 12

The World Series

While standing on the podium at Kauffman Stadium after the ALCS triumph, Ned Yost contrasted the 2015 pennant victory with the previous season. "Last year, we were happy to be there," Yost said. "This year, we expected to be here." Since before spring training the Royals had fixed their eyes on a return to the World Series. This confidence notwithstanding, winning a pennant is not easy. Repeating as pennant winners is even tougher. And losing a World Series by a narrow margin can have a demoralizing effect on a team. But not the Royals. Vanquishing two powerful rivals in the playoffs, Yost's boys had done it again. Kansas City became just the eighth team in baseball history to return to the World Series after losing Game 7 the year before.

"We've got unfinished business," said Mike Moustakas. "We don't want to lose the World Series again." But sports history is littered with determined teams that did not want to lose, but ended up losing anyway. Was there any reason to believe the Royals could avoid that fate? Eric Hosmer maintained that experience would make a difference this time. "Last year, we kind of didn't know what to expect coming into this," Hoz said. "This year, we definitely knew what we were getting ourselves into." He continued by pointing out the many late-inning comebacks his battle-tested team had engineered:

"So I think with all that installed in our minds over the last year, it just makes us a better team." Dayton Moore agreed, predicting that his team would remain tough-minded and mentally focused. Indeed, Royals players, coaches, and scouts wasted little time returning to work. "I'll probably watch 50 or 60 hours of video the next three days," Dave Eiland said after Game 6 of the ALCS.

While the Royals insisted they were ready to win the World Series, so too did their opponents—the New York Mets. The National League champs boasted arguably the top starting rotation in all of baseball. Their powerful offense led the NL in doubles and finished tied for third in home runs. Most ominously, they were riding a tidal wave of momentum— peaking at just the right time. Usually it is the hottest team in October, not the one with the best overall record, that wins the championship.

Like Kansas City the previous season, the Mets were expected to do little in 2015. The team had skidded through six-straight losing seasons. Manager Terry Collins had never led a big league team to the playoffs. In the preseason, sportsbooks listed the Mets as 28-1 longshots to win the World Series. And like the 2014 Royals, the Mets plodded through the first half of the season. But then the team caught fire. New York ascended to the top of the NL East with a 20-8 mark in August. In the NLDS, the Mets had to face the Dodgers and their formidable Cy Young duo of Clayton Kershaw and Zack Greinke. Even without home field advantage, New York prevailed in five. The Mets then had to face the red-hot Cubs in the NLCS. No problem. New York swept Chicago in four straight.

The Mets featured a three-headed rotation monster of Matt Harvey (2.71 ERA), Jacob deGrom (2.54 ERA), and Noah Syndergaard (3.24 ERA). All three fireballing starters averaged a strikeout per inning or better. No staff threw more pitches at 95-mph or faster than the Mets. Though New York's bullpen was not as deep as the Royals, it did possess one of the game's best closers in Jeurys Familia (43 saves, 1.85 ERA).

On the offensive side the Mets could deliver the pain, topping the National League in home runs in the season's second half. First baseman Lucas Duda led the team with 27 homers. Right fielder Curtis Granderson hit 26 long balls. And centerfielder Yoenis Cespedes had slashed a blistering .287/.337/.942 after a mid-season trade brought him from Detroit to New York. But the Mets' most dangerous hitter on the eve of the World Series was Daniel Murphy. The second baseman had homered in six straight postseason games, setting a MLB record.

Similar to Kansas City, New York did not lack in motivation. The National League pennant winners were seeking their first world championship since 1986. Often overshadowed in their own city by the celebrated Yankees, the Mets longed to recapture the glory days of Dwight Gooden, Gary Carter, and Darryl Strawberry.

Though bristling with offensive artillery and flamethrowing starters, New York's gloves represented a potential Achilles heel. Even at full strength, the Mets defense ranked no better than average. Cespedes, hampered by a shoulder injury, presented a potential liability in Kauffman's spacious outfield. And the Mets recently lost their everyday shortstop when Ruben Tejada suffered a broken leg in the NLDS.

Baseball pundits were divided in predicting the outcome of the Series matchup. Grantland's Ben Lindbergh favored the Royals, pointing out KC had a superior bullpen and a contact-savvy lineup that could handle fastballs. Moreover, four of the potential seven Series games would be played at Kauffman Stadium, where the Royals had a .630 winning percentage. Fellow Grantland scribe Jonah Keri liked the NL champs, arguing that the Mets lefty sluggers would feast upon the Royals inconsistent righty-laden rotation. Keri further maintained that the Mets starters wielded secondary pitches that would negate Kansas City's prowess against heat.

Similar to the baseball analysts, Vegas had a difficult time picking a favorite. Both teams possessed formidable strengths. Both teams had cleared difficult hurdles in the playoffs. And both teams were riding a wave of momentum. The sportsbooks Bovada and Oddshark set the Series odds as dead even. MyTopSportsbooks.com made the Royals a slight favorite. While neither team offered a large underdog payout, wagering that a naked fan would run onto the field during the series yielded 100 to 1 odds.

WORLD SERIES GAME 1

Ned Yost turned to his most reliable starter to open the Fall Classic. Edinson Volquez had pitched well in both of his ALCS starts, though a missed strike three call led to a brutal sixth inning in Game 5. Prior to that frame, he had been cruising. In the postseason thus far, Volquez had dialed up his fastball to the high 90s—four miles-per-hour faster than he threw during the regular season.

Terry Collins countered with Matt Harvey, the Dark Knight of Gotham. The right-hander had emerged two years earlier as one of the top young starters in the game, before a torn elbow ligament required Tommy John surgery in October 2013. Missing the following season, Harvey came back strong in 2015. But in early September his agent Scott Boras stirred controversy by announcing that, to avoid future injury, Harvey planned to shut down his season early when he reached a 180-inning limit (he had pitched 166 1/3 innings at that point). Mets fans were furious that their top pitcher would jeopardize his team's postseason chances to protect his own future earnings potential. Harvey later changed his position and remained in the rotation, winning each of his starts in the NLDS and NLCS. If he delivered in the World Series, the past controversy would become a forgotten footnote.

A sellout crowd packed into Kauffman Stadium. Not since Detroit's Navin Field hosted Game 1 in 1934 and 1935 had back-to-back World Series opened in the same ballpark. Pop singer Andy Grammer performed the national anthem. Hall of Famer George Brett threw out the ceremonial first pitch. The thermometer read 52 degrees on the pleasant overcast night. It was October 27th, a special day for both teams. On this date thirty years earlier, the Royals won Game 7 of the 1985 World Series. Exactly one year after that, the Mets defeated Boston in Game 7 to capture the 1986 Series.

A throng of blue-clad towel-waving fans cheered as the Royals emerged from the dugout to take the field. Volquez came out dealing. He sent the Mets down in order in the first, including a strike out of red-hot Daniel Murphy. Alcides Escobar led off for the Royals. Throughout the playoffs, he typically swung at the first pitch he saw. The World Series would be no different. Unloading on Harvey's opening fastball, Escobar hit a towering drive to deep left center. Yoenis Cespedes and Michael Conforto converged near the warning track, but neither had a good read. The ball caromed off Cespedes's leg and rolled away from the outfielders. By the time Conforto chased it down and returned it to the infield, Escobar had circled the bases with an inside-the-park home run. The crowd roared its approval of this unusual turn of events. Not since the first Fall Classic in 1903 had a batter led off a World Series game with an inside-the-park home run.

The score remained 1-0 until the top of the fourth. Murphy started the inning with a single to center. One out later, Lucas Duda drilled a hit into right, putting Mets at the corners. Catcher Travis d'Arnaud followed with a sharp grounder down the third base line. Mike Moustakas knocked it down, but had no play. Murphy scored, tying the game. The next inning Curtis Granderson hammered a Volquez fastball into the right field bullpen. In the sixth, Conforto delivered a sacrifice fly that plated Cespedes. After scoring in three consecutive innings, the Mets led 3-1.

Harvey meanwhile had retired eleven in a row. But as they had done all season, the Royals battled back. Ben Zobrist led off the sixth by smoking a double into the right field corner. Lorenzo Cain followed with an opposite-field single that put runners on the corners. Eric Hosmer then lifted a fly ball to center that scored Zobrist. After Cain stole second and Kendrys Morales grounded out, Moustakas lined a single into right center to deliver a clutch two-out RBI. The game was knotted at three.

Both managers went to their bullpens for the seventh. Neither team scored. With two outs in the eighth, Juan Lagares looped a hit up the middle off Kelvin Herrera. Two pitches later, the speedster stole second. Mets shortstop Wilmer Flores then chopped a two-hopper to first. Hosmer tried to backhand it, but missed. The ball bounded into the outfield and New York scored the go-ahead run.

The score remained 4-3 heading into the bottom of the ninth. Jeurys Familia stood atop the mound, ready to deploy his nasty sinkers to close out the Mets victory. The nearly untouchable reliever had not blown a save in three months. He retired Salvador Perez on a ground out. New York was about to win Game 1 on the road. And with Hosmer's error as the key play, what would be the psychological impact on him and his teammates? Alex Gordon batted. With the count 1-1, Familia tried a quick pitch—a hanging sinker that Gordon belted. The ball carried high and deep, landing well beyond the centerfield wall. As the left fielder rounded the bases, the stadium shook with a thunderous roar. Kansas City had tied the game.

Following this momentum shift, Wade Davis struck out the side in the top of the tenth. The Royals went down in order in the bottom of the frame. Neither team could score in the eleventh. For the twelfth, both managers summoned starting pitchers from the bullpen. Yost called upon Chris Young, who retired the Mets one-two-three. Collins chose veteran Bartolo Colon, a former Cy Young recipient who had won 14 games during the regular season. Though the Royals loaded the bases, they did not score. Both pitchers tossed a scoreless thirteenth as well.

The marathon contest entered the fourteenth inning. After Young delivered his third scoreless frame, Escobar led off the bottom half with a grounder to the left side. Mets third baseman David Wright knocked it down but threw wide to first, giving the Royals a baserunner. Zobrist followed by pulling a hit into right. Escobar advanced to third with nobody out. Colon intentionally walked Cain to load the bases. With 40,000 fans on their feet ready to erupt, Hosmer stepped to the plate. A little voice in his head whispered, "It's time for you to do your part." A potential goat a few innings earlier, the first baseman lifted a fly ball to right. Granderson caught it and fired home. Escobar crossed the plate before d'Arnaud could tag him. The Royals had captured Game 1.

Lasting more than five hours, it had been the longest World Series opener in baseball history. "It was a pretty cool way to get the World Series started," Danny Duffy said. His manager was not quite as thrilled about the length of the contest. "Two things you don't want in Game 1 of the World Series," Yost said afterwards. "One is to go 14 innings and the other is to lose." Hosmer was especially glad to avoid the second of those outcomes. "I was the happiest person in the stadium when Gordon homered," the first baseman said.

After the game, sad news tempered the atmosphere in the victors' clubhouse. Earlier in the day, Edinson Volquez's father Daniel died from heart disease complications. Royals officials learned this news about an hour before the game, but at the request of Edinson's wife Roandy they did not tell him. His family wanted him to pitch. Volquez learned the news after Yost removed him from the game. Soon after, he left with his wife and children to fly to the Dominican Republic. The thoughts and prayers of his Royals family went with him. Volquez was the third Royal to lose a parent during the season. "Words can't describe the pain I feel for Eddy tonight," said Game 1 winner Chris Young, whose father had died a month earlier.

WORLD SERIES GAME 2

After dropping the opening battle, the Mets looked to bounce back behind Jacob deGrom. A Rookie of the Year winner in 2014, the long-haired righty produced another stellar campaign his sophomore season. Representing the Mets in the 2015 All-

Star game, he finished the year with a 14-8 mark. His October was even more impressive when he went full deGrominator. Winning Game 1 and Game 5 of the NLDS, he contributed mightily to New York's vanquishing of the dangerous Dodgers. DeGrom continued his October dominance in the NLCS, shutting down the Cubs in Game 3. He headed into the World Series as the hottest starting pitcher on either team.

Johnny Cueto would toe the rubber for Kansas City. After his brilliant shutdown of Houston in Game 5 of the ALDS, the Royals believed that "Good Johnny" had arrived for the postseason. But a disastrous start in the ALCS in which Toronto shelled him for eight earned runs revived fears that Dayton Moore had bought a mid-season lemon. Heading into Game 2, Cueto represented the biggest question mark for the Royals.

Country star and Missouri native Sara Evans sang the national anthem. Honoring the military, the Royals selected three Medal of Honor recipients to throw out the ceremonial first pitch. All three veterans—retired Marine Colonel Don Ballard, retired Army Lieutenant Colonel Charles Hagemeister, and retired Army Colonel Roger Donlon—had served in the Vietnam War.

Both starting pitchers sent down the opposition one-two-three in the first inning. And so began this battle of the hair—deGrom's flowing locks versus Cueto's lengthy dreads. Early on, the contest looked to be a pitchers' duel. Cueto allowed an infield hit to Lucas Duda in the second, but otherwise shut down the Mets through the first three frames. DeGrom matched him, yielding only a harmless walk to Gordon in the third.

Granderson drew a walk to open the Mets fourth. One out later, Cueto walked Murphy. Cespedes then grounded to Moustakas who stepped on third for a force out, but could not complete a double play when his throw pulled Hosmer off first. New York still had runners at first and second. Duda followed by dropping a flare into left that resulted in a two-out RBI. Kansas City loaded the bases in the bottom of the frame, but could not answer.

Gordon opened the KC fifth by drawing a walk. Alex Rios lined a hit into left to put two men on. Escobar twice tried to drop a sacrifice bunt, but failed each time. With two strikes, the shortstop smacked a hanging slider into centerfield. Gordon scored and Kansas City still had men at first and second with nobody out. Zobrist advanced the runners to second and third with a ground out. After retiring Cain, deGrom looked like he would escape further damage. But Hosmer ripped a single up the middle, driving in Rios and Escobar. Hoz now had 27 career postseason RBIs, extending the Royals franchise record he set the night before. After Kendrys Morales laced a single into right, Moustakas followed with an RBI grounder that plated Hosmer. The productive inning put Kansas City up 4-1.

Now with a lead, Cueto bore down even harder. The dreadlocked one retired the Mets in order in the sixth, seventh, and eighth. To ensure their starter had a shot at a complete game, Kansas City piled on three more runs in the eighth. An opposite-field hit from Gordon, a sacrifice fly from Paulo Orlando, and a triple from Escobar had driven home the tallies.

With the cheering crowd on its feet, Cueto came out to pitch the ninth. Granderson grounded out to Zobrist. Wright grounded out to Moustakas. Following a walk to Murphy, Cespedes ended the game by flying out to Orlando in right. A question mark heading into the contest, Cueto had tossed a two-hitter to provide an emphatic answer to his doubters. It was the first World Series complete game from an American League pitcher since 1991.

"That's what they brought me here for, was to help win a World Series," Cueto said after the game. Displaying masterful command, the right-hander hit the strike zone with an array of different pitches. And he disrupted the Mets timing by using quick pitches and delayed deliveries. Yost noted that Cueto performed much better at Kauffman. "He loves our fans," the manager said. "He feeds off their energy."

On the offensive side, it was another case of the Royals "keep the line moving" attack. Despite facing 98-mph fastballs, Kansas City batters swung and missed only three times against deGrom. "We find ways to just keep putting the ball in play until you find holes," Yost said. Hitting coach Dale Sveum further explained that swinging early, shortening up, and being aggressive at the plate was a team mindset. "When we get to crunch time, we can't strike out," Sveum said, "because we're not going to walk very much."

The Royals led the series two games to none. More than 80 percent of past World Series teams in that position went on to win the title. But the 1986 Mets were one of the teams to come back from such a deficit. With the Series now shifting to New York, the NL champs insisted the Fall Classic was far from over. "By no means are we done," Lucas Duda said. "We've created a hole for ourselves, but we've been here before."

WORLD SERIES GAME 3

The teams flew to New York to play Game 3 on Friday evening, October 30th. Much Royals history had transpired in The Big Apple. In 1976 Yankee first baseman Chris Chambliss hit a ninth-inning home run in the decisive game of the ALCS to crush Kansas City's pennant hopes. Two years later, Cy Young winner Ron Guidry ended another KC postseason in the Bronx. In Game 3 of the 1980 ALCS, George Brett blasted a three-run homer into the upper deck at Yankee Stadium to propel Kansas City to its first World Series. In July 1983 another Brett homer in New York ignited a controversy that became known as the Pine Tar Game.

All of those events occurred against the Yankees. In October 2015 the Royals returned to the same city, but faced a different team. Aside from the Royals' disastrous trade of David Cone in 1987, Kansas City and the Mets had little significant history. That was bound to change over the next three days. For New York, playing at Citi Field offered the chance to turn the World Series around. For Yost's boys, they had an opportunity to finish off an epic quest to claim the rings.

Collins turned to his third flamethrower, Noah Syndergaard. Nicknamed "Thor," the 6-foot-6 rookie with Nordic blond locks could hit 100 mph on the radar gun. Complimenting this heat with a wicked secondary selection of curves, changes, and sliders, the right-hander had struck out 166 batters in 150 innings during the regular season. He continued this dominance in the playoffs with 20 strikeouts in 13 innings against the Dodgers and the Cubs. In the NLCS Syndergaard defeated the best pitcher in baseball, Cubs soon-to-be-named Cy Young winner Jake Arrieta.

Yost countered with his own bazooka-armed starter. Winless in the playoffs thus far, Yordano Ventura looked for a repeat of his last World Series performance. With his team facing elimination in the 2014 Fall Classic, the right-hander tossed seven shutout innings in Game 6 to propel the Royals past the Giants. Despite his lapses in the 2015 postseason, with 21 strikeouts in 17 2/3 innings against the Astros and Blue Jays, Ventura showed he could still throw fire.

Throughout the postseason, Kansas City leadoff hitter Alcides Escobar consistently swung at the first pitch of the game. This usually yielded positive results, most notably his inside-the-park home run in Game 1. Fox announcers, national sportswriters, talk-show hosts, bloggers, and fans across the nation endlessly wondered aloud why opposing hurlers would throw a first-pitch strike to Escobar. Hearing this message, Syndergaard promised he had "a few tricks" for the KC leadoff batter.

After Billy Joel sang the national anthem, Thor took the hill as the eerie theme from the 1978 horror film *Halloween* echoed through the windy ballpark. The big Met fired his first pitch, a 98-mph fastball, high and inside past Escobar's head. The shortstop ducked, dropping to his backside in the dirt. The crowd roared its approval. Royals players took a different view, yelling unpleasantries at Syndergaard. As he intended, the rookie had established his presence with authority. Escobar struck out swinging.

It would take more than a brushback pitch to disrupt the Royals though. Batting second, Zobrist smashed a Syndergaard fastball deep to center, where it short-hopped the wall. Cain followed with a check-swing infield single that put runners on the corners. Hosmer then chopped a high bouncer to first, adding to his record postseason RBI total. Kansas City went up 1-0.

The lead would not last. Granderson led off the Mets first by beating out a grounder that Zobrist fielded in shallow right. David Wright then blasted a Ventura fastball deep into the seats in left center. The Royals quickly answered. Perez and Gordon opened the second with back-to-back singles. Rios then ripped a hit into left. Perez scored as Gordon rounded second and raced toward third. Michael Conforto fired to Wright, who applied the tag. Umpire Gary Cederstrom made the safe call, but a video replay review overturned the ruling. New York had recorded a big out. As Rios took his lead off second, Ventura stepped to the plate. Since this game was at a National League ballpark, the pitchers had to bat. Though hitless in his six regular season at-bats, Ventura laid down a perfect bunt that advanced the runner to third. With Escobar at the plate, a Syndergaard curve slipped under d'Arnaud's mitt and rolled to the backstop. Rios raced home and Kansas City had reclaimed the lead 3-2.

Leading off the bottom of the third, Syndergaard, a .209 hitter during the regular season, lined an 0-2 pitch into right. Granderson made this mistake hurt by driving a fastball over the right field wall. An inning later, the Mets put runners at second and third with nobody out. Conforto then chopped an infield hit that scored a run. After Ventura retired Flores on a pop out, Yost brought in Danny Duffy. Kansas City escaped the inning with no further damage, but now trailed 5-3.

After a shaky start, Syndergaard found his groove. He retired the Royals in order in the third, fourth, and fifth innings. In the sixth, Kansas City loaded the bases with two outs, but Thor hammered down the threat by inducing a groundout from Rios.

Looking to keep the game close, Yost sent Franklin Morales to pitch the sixth. Hijinks ensued. With one run in and Mets at the corners, Granderson grounded back to the mound. After fielding the ball, Morales danced around, unsure where to throw. He finally decided on second, but the ball sailed wide and the runner was safe. Based loaded. Yost brought in Herrera to try to douse the fire. He gave up a single, a walk, and a sac fly to plate three more runs. New York led 9-3. The Mets bullpen preserved the victory with three scoreless innings.

After the game, Syndergaard's opening pitch was the lead story. He said he wanted to make a statement that the Royals could not get too aggressive with him. "My intent on that pitch was to make them uncomfortable," Syndergaard said, "and I feel like I did just that." Though it fired up the Kansas City dugout, Thor apparently achieved his objective. After giving up three early runs, he shut down the visitors, striking out six. "He came through exactly as we expected," Terry Collins said.

The Royals nonetheless remained confident in defeat. Ventura still expected to finish off the series in New York. "There's two more games here," the pitcher said, "and I know that we can get it done here." Ventura's outing nonetheless left significant questions. After starting the game firing 97-mph heaters, why did his velocity drop to the low 90s? And why did he lose his command by the third inning? If the Series went to seven games, Ventura would be the starter in the decisive winner-take-all contest. With his 6.43 ERA in the 2015 postseason, a Royals championship could depend on him finding the answers to these questions.

A potential Game 7 was a long way off. Both teams turned their attention to the next day. The winner of Game 4 would claim the driver's seat for this series.

WORLD SERIES GAME 4

Though the Royals still led the World Series, two ominous historical parallels hovered above them. With a two-to-one-game lead on the road, they now found themselves in the same situation they were in after Game 3 against the Giants a year earlier. Kansas City dropped three of the next four to lose the World Series. More troubling for the Boys in Blue, the Mets were now on track to repeat the 1986 World Series. In that Fall Classic, New York lost the first game by one run, lost the second game by six runs, and won the third game by six runs. The 2015 results thus far matched the exact same margins. Twenty-nine years earlier, the Mets won three of the next four games to capture the world championship.

Ned Yost was more interested in recent history—the postseason outings of Chris Young. The Royals Game 4 starter had turned in a sparkling 2.31 ERA this postseason. And he was the winning pitcher in the marathon Game 1. The towering hurler had come through time and time again during the regular season when the Kansas City rotation threatened to fall apart. In the biggest start of Young's career, his team needed him to stem the growing tide of Mets momentum.

For the second game in a row, Collins gave the ball to a rookie. A minor leaguer for most of 2015, twenty-four-year-old Steven Matz had made only six regular season starts for New York. But the Long Island native posted impressive numbers, finishing 4-0 with a 2.86 ERA. While the lefty did not throw as hard as the other Mets starters, he changed speeds effectively to get batters out.

Though both pitchers were the number-four men in their respective rotations, they looked like aces early on. After a leadoff hit by Escobar, Matz allowed just one other harmless single while shutting out the Royals over the first three innings. Looking to match him, Young sent the Mets down in order in the first and second innings. In the bottom of the third, however, Conforto led off by launching a fastball into the upper deck in right. Wilmer Flores then lined a single into center. On Young's next delivery, the runner advanced to second on a wild pitch. Matz laid down a bunt to send Flores to third with just one out. Granderson followed by lofting a fly to right. Moving in, Rios looked to have a shot at cutting down the runner at the plate. But the KC outfielder thought there were two outs. After making the catch, he took a couple steps before realizing his mistake. It was too late. The mental lapse allowed Flores to race home with New York's second run.

Both pitchers breezed through a one-two-three fourth. With one out in the fifth, Salvador Perez hit a fly into center that dropped in front of Cespedes. When the outfielder misplayed the ball, Perez cruised into second. Gordon followed with an RBI single to cut the Mets lead in half. After Rios flew out, the pitcher was due to bat. Looking for a big inning, Yost sent Kendrys Morales to pinch hit for Young. The DH grounded a single up the middle, giving the Royals two men on with two out. But Escobar flew out to end the inning.

Danny Duffy entered the game to pitch the fifth. Conforto welcomed him by driving a breaking ball over the wall for his second homer of the game. New York had increased its lead to two again. Zobrist led off the Royals' next at-bat by ripping a double to the wall in left center. It was his eighth two-bagger of the postseason, tying a MLB record. Cain rolled a grounder up the middle to send Zobrist home. Kansas City had cut the lead to 3-2.

The score remained unchanged heading into the eighth. Just six outs away from tying up the Series, Collins called upon Tyler Clippard to preserve the lead. The veteran right-hander had closed for Oakland prior to a mid-season trade that brought him to the Mets. In New York he pitched great in August as a set-up man, but struggled down the stretch in September. Clippard retired Escobar on a groundout, before walking Zobrist and Cain to put the tying run in scoring position. Collins summoned Familia and his 0.75 postseason ERA to get the last five outs. The power-throwing closer won an apparent victory when Hosmer chopped a slow bouncer to the right side. But the charging Daniel Murphy missed the ball, which rolled under his glove into shallow right. Zobrist scored and the Royals had runners at the corners. Moustakas followed by grounding a hit into right that scored Cain. Perez then lined an opposite-field single that sent Hosmer home. The Royals led 5-3.

With the tables turned, Yost unleashed his cyborg to finish off the Mets. Wade Davis shot down all three batters he faced in the eighth. The closer opened the ninth by striking out Wright. Murphy provided a glimmer of hope for the Citi Field fans by shooting a single past Moustakas. Cespedes then lined a hit into right. The Mets had the tying run on base with the powerful Lucas Duda at the plate. With the game on the line, The Terminator activated. Swinging at an 0-1 pitch, Duda flared a broken-bat looper to third. Moustakas gloved it and noticed that Cespedes had wandered far off the bag at first. Moose fired across the diamond to complete the game-ending double play.

Much like Game 1, the Mets had let a victory slip away. Or was it a case of the Royals taking it? The outcome marked Kansas City's sixth multi-run comeback in the postseason, setting a Major League Baseball record. "There's just a belief amongst the guys that it doesn't matter what the score is, what the lead is, what the deficit is," Chris Young said. "The guys just believe that they're going to find a way to get it done." Yost agreed, commenting that at no point did his players think they were going to lose the game.

And so on Halloween night, an error from the NLCS MVP haunted the Mets. "I just misplayed it," Murphy said. "It went under my glove. They made us pay for it." Like the Astros and Blue Jays before them, the Mets had learned that opening the door for a confident, experienced team that thrives on putting the ball in play is not a good idea. "That's the important thing about this ballclub," Zobrist said. "Guys understand how to hit and approach at-bats with the best hitting philosophy."

The Royals now stood one game away from the championship that had so cruelly eluded them a year earlier. With a commanding 3-1 lead, Yost's boys just needed to take one of the next three contests. But momentum can change quickly in a short series. "This game will show you something new every day," observed Danny Duffy. Both teams hoped that statement was true. The Mets hoped to find a new way to beat Kansas City. The Royals hoped to claim a new trophy.

WORLD SERIES GAME 5

In baseball history a dozen major league teams had come back from a three-games-to-one deficit to win a postseason series. If there was a team capable of doing that in 2015 it was the Mets. Their fearsome trio of power arms—Harvey, deGrom, and Syndergaard—were lined up for such a run. A few days earlier in the NLCS, New York had swept the hottest team in baseball in four straight. If the Mets could win at home in Game 5, they would face two question mark Royals starters (Cueto and Ventura) in the final two games. This series was not over.

The pitching matchup would be a rematch of the opening contest: Volquez vs. Harvey. Kansas City's starter had rejoined his team a day earlier after attending his father's funeral in the Dominican Republic. Despite the added emotional challenge to what was already a high-pressure game, Volquez stated he was ready. "I'm pretty sure my dad is going to be proud of me when I pitch tomorrow on the mound," he said after arriving in New York.

For Matt Harvey, the subject of much controversy during the season, he now faced the elevated stakes of pitching a must-win game. In the opening contest, fatigue and a wariness of the Royals' fastball-hitting prowess led him to reduce his reliance on heaters. He threw a fastball on only 38 percent of his pitches that game. During the regular season, the Dark Knight had fired in fastballs 60 percent of the time. With his team's back to the wall, could Harvey summon the reserve in his final start of the year to again become the flamethrower that had made him so feared?

Gotham's superhero deployed all his bat-weapons in the first, striking out two and holding the Royals scoreless. Before throwing his first pitch in the bottom of the inning, Volquez drew his father's initials on the mound. Edinson later said he felt his dad's presence with him on the field. Leading off for the

Mets, Curtis Granderson wasted little time putting his team on top. Unloading on a hanging 0-2 change-up, he drove the ball over the wall in right center. Met fans buzzed with hope that this would be their team's night to get back in the Series.

This impression looked even more likely as the game progressed. Moustakas reached on an error in the second and Volquez singled in the third, but Kansas City could not score. And Harvey just seemed to get stronger. Like Batman dispatching the Joker, Penguin, and Riddler, he struck out the side in the fourth. Gordon drew a walk in the fifth, but Harvey struck out three more. A Zobrist single was all KC could manage in the sixth as the shutout remained intact.

Volquez also pitched magnificently. After the leadoff homer, he did not allow another hit through five innings. But Granderson led off the New York sixth with a walk. Wright grounded a single into left. Hosmer then misplayed a hot smash from Murphy to load the bases with nobody out. Volquez got Cespedes to pop out, but Duda followed with a fly ball that plated Granderson. Volquez retired the next batter to limit the damage to one run. Kansas City, however, now trailed 2-0—a lead that seemed much larger the way Harvey was pitching.

Invoking unwanted memories of the fiendish ace the Royals faced in Game 5 a year ago, the Dark Knight remained in command. Moose singled in the seventh, but could not advance past first. After Harvey retired the side in order in the eighth, the Royals were down to their final three outs. The Mets could smell victory and a chance to travel to Kansas City for Game 6.

With only a two-run lead, Terry Collins prepared to send his shutdown closer Jeurys Familia to pitch the ninth. Harvey rejected this plan. "No way," he told his manager. Having dominated all night, Batman wanted the complete-game shutout. Collins acceded to his pitcher's demands. When Harvey emerged from the dugout for the top of the ninth, the crowd erupted in a roar that carried across Queens. Gotham's hero would finish the job, reigniting a city's hopes.

That storyline, however, did not quite work for the Royals. As they tended to do, the Boys in Blue rewrote the script calling for a rousing New York victory. Leading off, Cain battled through a seven-pitch at-bat to draw a walk. Up in the stands, George Brett said, "I've seen this movie before." Taking off on the next pitch, Cain stole second. Hosmer then smoked a double into the left field corner. Cain crossed the plate, and the Royals had the tying run at second. Collins brought in Familia to preserve the now slim lead. Moustakas pulled a grounder to the right side, advancing Hosmer to third.

Salvador Perez stepped to the plate. Just like in the World Series a year earlier, he batted in the ninth with the tying run ninety feet away. But this time there was just one out. The catcher needed only a fly ball to drive in the run. With the count 1-0, Familia jammed Perez with an inside fastball that broke his bat. The resulting soft liner bounced to the left of David Wright, who fielded it and looked back at Hosmer shuffling a few steps off the bag. When the Met third baseman threw to first, Hoz bolted for the plate. This was a foolhardy move that would end the game when Lucas Duda fired home to gun him down. It was a huge baserunning gaffe that would go down as one of the biggest blunders of the Series.

Except that it worked. Hosmer was aware from scouting reports that a back injury had reduced Wright's throwing velocity. And he knew that, when rushed, Duda did not have the most accurate throwing arm. The Met first baseman's hurried throw home sailed wide, past d'Arnaud's glove. Hosmer slid headfirst across the plate with the tying run. Ninety feet attained.

The Royals bounded out of their dugout, reenergized by yet another comeback. Demoralized Mets fans slumped in their seats. Herrera retired the home team in order in the bottom of the ninth. The game entered extra innings—a new hope for one team, an impending nightmare for the other.

Both sides went down in order in the tenth. Hosmer singled and stole second in the eleventh, but Kansas City could not score. Luke Hochevar yielded a walk in the bottom of the frame, before completing his second scoreless inning.

Collins brought in Addison Reed to pitch the twelfth. Arriving in New York via a trade at the end of August, the big right-hander did not allow an earned run the entire month of September. In the postseason thus far, the reliever had posted a suffocating 1.35 ERA.

Perez greeted Reed by slicing a blooper that landed just fair inside the right field line. Yost sent Jarrod Dyson to run for the burly catcher. Dyson promptly showed what speed can do by stealing second. Gordon pulled a grounder to first, advancing the runner to third. With the pitcher due to bat next, Yost sent Christian Colon to the plate. Though a hero in the previous year's Wild Card game, the reserve infielder was making his first plate appearance in the 2015 postseason. He had not batted in nearly a full month. Ahead 1-2 in the count and looking for a strikeout, Reed fired to the plate. Colon drilled the slider into left—once again he was a hero. Dyson crossed the plate, giving Kansas City the lead.

Down in the visitors' bullpen, The Terminator sprang to life. He would need just three outs to complete the World Series victory. But the Royals batters were not through moving the line. Murphy booted a Paulo Orlando grounder, putting runners at first and second. Escobar then doubled down the left field line, scoring Colon. Reed intentionally walked Zobrist to load the bases. Collins brought in Bartolo Colon in a desperate attempt to keep the game close. Cain ripped a bases-clearing double into left center. Kansas City had broken open the game, 7-2.

Wade Davis came on to deliver the coup de grace. He struck out Duda. He struck out d'Arnaud. Conforto singled to left to prolong his team's season by one more at-bat. Flores stepped to the plate, hoping to avoid being the last batter of the year. Davis struck him out looking. After catching the final strike, Drew Butera threw off his mask and ran out to embrace Davis. The Boys in Blue converged on the infield to celebrate. The Kansas City Royals had won the 2015 World Series.

It had been 368 days since the team had endured a heartbreaking season-ending defeat.

And now, finished business.

Catcher Salvador Perez visits reliever Kelvin Herrera on the mound during a game against Oakland at Kauffman Stadium in April 2015.
Peter G. Aiken-USA TODAY Sports

Yordano Ventura and Johnny Cueto work out before a game against the White Sox. Cueto helped the younger pitcher regain his effectiveness during the 2015 stretch run.
Peter G. Aiken-USA TODAY Sports

Lorenzo Cain rounds third against Toronto. Batting .307 with 16 homers, 72 RBIs, and 28 stolen bases, Cain finished third in AL MVP voting in 2015.
Dan Hamilton-USA TODAY Sports

Wade Davis pitches in the ninth inning of Game 5 of the ALDS.
Peter G. Aiken-USA TODAY Sports

Ben Zobrist congratulates Kendrys Morales after the DH slammed a two-run homer against Tampa Bay in August. *Kim Klement-USA TODAY Sports*

Alex Gordon bats for the Omaha Storm Chasers during his rehabilitation assignment in
August 2015. *Ron Kalkwarf*

Shortstop Alcides Escobar completes a double
play against the Blue Jays in Game 5 of the ALCS.
John E. Sokolowski-USA TODAY Sports

Omar Infante on the Crown
Vision video board at The K.

The Kauffman Stadium grounds crew unfurls the tarp after rain halted play before the third inning of ALDS Game 1. *Ron Kalkwarf*

Right fielder Alex Rios on the video board at Kauffman Stadium.

Mike Moustakas belts a home run in Game 6 of the ALCS against Toronto. *Peter G. Aiken-USA TODAY Sports*

Alex Gordon ties Game 1 of the World Series with a
clutch ninth-inning home run.
Peter G. Aiken-USA TODAY Sports

Chris Young tossed three scoreless relief innings
to pick up the win in Game 1 of the World Series.
John Rieger-USA TODAY Sports

Edinson Volquez pitches in Game 5
of the World Series.
*Julie Jacobson/Pool Photo via USA
TODAY Sports*

Manager Ned Yost and owner David Glass with the Commissioner's Trophy after the Royals World Series victory. *Al Bello/Pool Photo via USA TODAY Sports*

Salvador Perez on stage with GM Dayton Moore at Union Station in Kansas City during the World Series victory celebration. *Denny Medley-USA TODAY Sports*

Chapter 13

Blue November

The end of a baseball season. It means different things to different teams. Just three years earlier the Royals season ended on October 3, 2012. Failing to score against Detroit that evening, Kansas City dropped its 90th game. The Boys in Blue had posted nine straight losing seasons. Completing his third year as Royals manager, Ned Yost had yet to prevent a 90-loss campaign. Alex Gordon was on that team. So too were Hosmer, Perez, Moustakas, Escobar, Cain, Dyson, Hochevar, Herrera, Guthrie, and Holland. They and their teammates departed The K to ponder a franchise playoff drought that approached three decades.

Three years later. November 1, 2015. A very different end to the Royals season. Champagne. Goggles. A trophy with all the flags on it. Yost and his boys celebrated a world title in the visitors' clubhouse at Citi Field. Baseball commissioner Rob Manfred presented David Glass with the championship hardware. "Guys, mission accomplished," the owner told his team gathered before him. Next to take the microphone, Dayton Moore also praised the players. "They got great hearts to play," the GM said. "They represent the game of baseball first class." Ned Yost expressed similar thoughts in his postgame interview. "So to be able to win this is very, very special, with this group of guys," the manager said, "with their character, with their heart, with their passion, with the energy that they bring every single day. I mean, they leave everything on the field."

Salvador Perez was named World Series MVP, an honor that netted him a trophy and a 2016 Chevrolet Camaro. Battered and bruised from a season of foul tips, backswings, and beanings, the hardy catcher batted .364 with three runs scored and two RBIs during the Series. He also threw out two of three potential base stealers, and guided a pitching staff that kept the Mets in check. Salvy recalled his early years together with his teammates. "We've got the same group, almost the same group, when I played my first year in 2007 in Arizona, the Rookie League," Perez said. "It's amazing now to win a World Series and see the same guys with you." Reporters asked about the pain he endured after two grueling seasons of catching the most games in baseball. They also inquired about the heartbreak of popping out to end the 2014 Series. The gregarious backstop dismissed any past pains and disappointments. "Kansas City is Number 1," Perez said. "Who cares about what happened last year?"

For the Boys in Blue, this evening would have been hard to imagine just three years earlier. "Words can't even describe how awesome this feels right now," Eric Hosmer said. "Couldn't have done it with a better group of guys." Lorenzo Cain expressed similar feelings. "I mean this entire clubhouse, front office, fans, they're all amazing," the outfielder said. "We continue to push no matter if it's not in our favor, continue to fight as a team."

The fight had been even more difficult for Kansas City's Game 5 starter. Just days after his father's funeral, Edinson Volquez willed himself to remain calm and focused on the mound. The right-hander held the Mets to just two hits and one earned run over six innings. "I couldn't have been prouder of that kid," Glass said. "He really stood tall tonight." The encouragement and support of his teammates and other members of the Royals family helped Volquez. "You feel a lot of pain in your heart," the pitcher said, "and then you come to the ballpark and you feel a lot of support and a lot of love when you need it."

Thanks to Volquez's pitching, Kansas City remained within striking distance of the Mets in Game 5. But they trailed by two runs in the ninth against a pitcher who had owned them all night. No problem. The Royals coolly went about their work like they expected to win. Dayton Moore had a feeling it would happen. So did Chris Young. After Cain led off the ninth with a walk, the pitcher said, "Here we go again." And after the Royals evened things up, Yost could smell victory. "So really, after we tied it, I felt totally relaxed," the manager told reporters. "I even said, 'My heart should be beating faster than it is.'"

The postgame party at Citi Field topped all previous celebrations during the season. Jeremy Guthrie pumped up the team one more time. Shouts and whoops followed. Champagne showers drenched the victorious players. Braving the deluge, reporters interviewed the jubilant champions. Movie star and Kansas City native Paul Rudd joined the fun. The Royals doused him. Finally, as dawn approached, the players, coaches, and their families left the scene of their greatest baseball triumph. While on the plane, Yost received a congratulatory call from President Barack Obama. Oh how things had changed since October 2012.

A GOOD DAY FOR A PARADE

The 2015 Royals had played their last baseball game of the year, but they still had one more team event to attend. On Tuesday, November 3rd, Kansas City held a parade to honor the World Series champions. Though the Royals had played in front of sold-out ballparks all season, they had never seen a crowd like the one that gathered that day. With a city population of 467,000, planners estimated that about 250,000 would show up. That number proved to be a bit low. Somewhere around 800,000 people descended upon downtown Kansas City to line the parade route and gather at Union Station.

The players and their families rolled through the downtown streets as blue-clad throngs, standing two-dozen deep in places, waved and cheered. "Every street corner you turned, you'd see a flood of people," Hosmer said, "then you'd look past a building and see even more." Schools and businesses closed. The mass of humanity caused multiple traffic jams. Many fans parked their cars miles away and walked. Some even left their vehicles on the side of the interstate. The massive blue swarm comprised the largest crowd to attend an event in Kansas City's (and perhaps Missouri's) history.

And it is history that helps explain the reason for this huge turnout. Royals fans had endured a dark age of nearly three decades. Fresh humiliations and frustrations came each year. Great players traded away as they entered their prime. Losing streaks that produced 100-loss seasons. Embarrassed team employees hiding their badges after leaving the ballpark. Finally, a breakthrough in 2014—but even that epic season ended in heartbreak. This November parade was a franchise saying thank you to its longsuffering loyal fans. And the children waving flags, the teens with painted faces, the men with blue-dyed mustaches, the women with blue wigs—they and everyone else packed into downtown KC enjoyed every minute of it.

The parade vehicles deposited the players at Union Station, where the team assembled on a stage. There, the Boys in Blue fully realized the scope of their fans' devotion. "It was, like, wave after wave of people," Hosmer said. "And then, up on the stage, you could probably go back, like, five football fields, and it was all people in Royal blue."

Wearing dark hoodies that read "Thanks Kansas City," the players took turns at the microphone to address the masses. Gordon told the crowd they were they best fans in the world. Escobar fondly recalled the trade that brought him to the Royals. Perez took a selfie with his *hermanito* Cain. Volquez predicted a Royals return to the World Series in 2016. But the speech of the day came from Jonny Gomes. Acquired in a trade with little more than a month left in the season, the bearded outfielder only had five hits for the Royals and did not appear in a single postseason game. But the veteran still made his presence felt. Strutting back and forth on stage with a U.S. flag like pro wrestler Hacksaw Jim Duggan, Gomes fired up the masses with his enthusiastic monologue. "Hey guess what, Cy Young winner, not on our team. Beat him! Rookie of the year, not on our team. We beat him! MVP of the whole league ... sorry guys, not on our team, but we beat that guy too!" His teammates clapped and cheered after every comment. "Do you know why we beat 'em?" Gomes asked. "Because all y'all people had our backs!" After his speech, the team mobbed Gomes while the jubilant crowd started chanting, "Thank you, Royals!"

The World Series festivities did not end with the parade. After the event, Jimmy Fallon sent a private jet to fly Salvador Perez and Eric Hosmer, along with the championship trophy, to New York to appear on NBC's *The Tonight Show*. The last time the Royals won the World Series, host Johnny Carson interviewed Series MVP Bret Saberhagen. After Fallon discussed the Royals victory with Perez and Hosmer, Saberhagen showed up to poke fun at a cheesy "rapping" Ford commercial he made thirty years earlier. The show ended with Salvy dousing Fallon with one of his trademark ice water baths.

Over on ABC, Mike Moustakas, Jeremy Guthrie, and Drew Butera joined television star and Royals fan Eric Stonestreet on *Jimmy Kimmel Live!* Stonestreet and Kimmel had made a bet on the World Series outcome, in which the loser would get shot by paintballs in a bouncy house. Like James Caan in *The Godfather*, Kimmel was riddled with paint bullets fired by Stonestreet and his Royal friends. To the victors go the spoils.

WHAT WENT RIGHT?

A year earlier, the World Series left the Royals and their fans asking, *What went wrong?* Twelve months later, Kansas City's postseason performance spawned a different question: *What went right?*

One of the team's most celebrated strengths, the bullpen played a key role in the Royals' October success. In sixteen postseason games, Kansas City starters pitched 83 1/3 innings with a batter-friendly 4.97 ERA. The Royals bullpen, on the other hand, pitched 64 2/3 innings with a stingy 2.51 ERA. Though Kansas City starters produced some notable gems in the postseason, they often exited with their team trailing. The KC relievers, in contrast, consistently clamped down on the opposition. This proved crucial as the Royals tried to battle back from late-inning deficits.

Greg Holland's season-ending injury shackled the H-D-H beast that had proved so ferocious during the 2014 playoffs. But an equally formidable monster emerged from the KC pen in October 2015. Luke Hochevar tossed 10 2/3 innings in the postseason without yielding a run. Kelvin Herrera again brought the flames, allowing just a single earned run over 13 2/3 postseason innings. And Wade Davis could not be touched, allowing zero earned runs over 10 and 2/3 innings. Along the way, The Terminator picked up a win and four saves.

Accompanying this dominant bullpen was a superior defense. Since 2013, Kansas City's gloves had led the major leagues in defensive runs saved and ultimate zone rating. The Royals exploited this fielding advantage to full effect during their championship run. Through the three rounds of the postseason, KC's opponents made nine errors compared to just three for the Royals. And in all three rounds, opponent miscues contributed to Kansas City rallies: Correa's whiff of Morales's bouncer in Game 4 of the ALDS; Bautista and Goin's misplay of Zobrist's pop fly in Game 2 of the ALCS; and Murphy's whiff of Hosmer's grounder in Game 4 of the World Series.

The Royals offense provided the third major factor behind their Series triumph. Leading off, Alcides Escobar hit safely in 15 straight games—the longest streak in a single postseason in MLB history. He finished with a .329 postseason batting average. Ben Zobrist also batted over .300, with eight doubles and a .515 slugging average. Kendrys Morales and Salvador

Perez each blasted four postseason home runs. And Eric Hosmer became an RBI machine. Though he batted only .212 in the playoffs and World Series, if there were men on base he delivered, driving in 17 runs in 16 games. As a team, Kansas City slashed a sizzling .349/.405/.450 with runners in scoring position. And Yost's boys continued to use speed as a weapon. The Royals' 14 postseason stolen bases doubled that of their opponents.

Beyond the numbers though is perhaps the most important factor explaining the Royals triumph. This team possessed a relentless, never-quit mentality that propelled them through comeback after comeback. Matt Harvey may have fashioned himself as the Dark Knight, but Kansas City was the unconquerable Justice League. No matter what the villains threw at them, the blue superheroes could not be vanquished. Kansas City came back from multiple-run deficits in seven of their eleven postseason wins—a baseball record. Three times in the World Series New York led in the eighth inning or later, only to succumb to a Kansas City rally. Houston and Toronto experienced similar frustrations. In the first six innings of Kansas City's sixteen postseason games, the opposition outscored the Royals 55 to 39. In the seventh inning and after, the Boys in Blue outscored their opponents by a mind-boggling 51 to 11 margin.

As noted by Yost and his players, the Royals never-give-up mindset dated back to their comeback from a 7-3 eighth-inning deficit in the 2014 Wild Card game. "I think from that point on, it's just been a different club," said Hosmer. "It just created a whole new swagger about us…." Perez agreed. "We never quit," the catcher said. "We always compete to the last out." The aggressive philosophy of hitting coach Dale Sveum helped cement this attitude, which fueled the team's penchant for rallying. The originator of the "keep the line moving" mantra, he impressed upon his players the need to make contact. "You get three outs in an inning, and if you strike out for two of those outs, your odds of coming back aren't going to be very good,"

Sveum said. "But if you put three balls in play, something might fall and you keep the line moving."

Added to all of the above was the motivation factor. The 2015 Royals were on a mission. "And when you get to the top of the mountain and you fall, and then next year people are saying you're going to finish third in your division … it makes you determined to prove everybody wrong," Hosmer said. "And that desire helped carry this team through the grind of the season." During the postseason, the Royals proved especially relentless in their quest to take care of unfinished business. Five straight singles in the eighth inning of Game 4 of the ALDS. Cain scoring from first on a single in Game 6 of the ALCS. Hosmer breaking for the plate in the ninth inning of World Series Game 5. Relentless. Relentless. Relentless.

Finally, there is Ned Yost. About to be run out of town a year earlier when the Royals fell behind in the Wild Card game, his team's comeback against Oakland that night began his legacy. The drive to the 2014 World Series. The return to the World Series twelve months later. Through the bad seasons and good, he always believed in his players. In 2015 he acquired the ring. He silenced the legion of critics that once called for his head. Will the haters continue to hate? Probably. But for those who still doubt the genius of Ned Yost there is this statistic: His postseason managerial record is 22-9. The corresponding .710 winning percentage is the best ever among MLB managers with at least 20 postseason games.

Sorry Joe Torre, Sparky Anderson, Billy Martin, Casey Stengel, Connie Mack, and Joe McCarthy. You and all the other managerial legends of baseball history have been Yosted!

GREATEST ROYALS TEAM EVER?

Near the conclusion of the November 3rd celebration at Union Station, George Brett took the microphone and addressed the crowd. The Hall of Famer proclaimed that the players standing behind him on stage were the greatest Royals team ever—even better than his own championship squad. The crowd roared its approval.

The proclamation is understandable. It was a day to celebrate the conquering heroes. But Brett's statement does raise an interesting question. Which Royals team is in fact the best in franchise history?

The most obvious past contender for greatest Royals team is the 1985 squad that won the World Series. That squad had a better hitter (Brett) and a better starting pitcher (Saberhagen) than any member of the 2015 Royals. But, despite one of Brett's best seasons (.335, 30 HRs, 112 RBIs) and a franchise-record 36 homers from first baseman Steve Balboni, the 1985 team could not match the overall offense of the 2015 Royals. Yost's team outslashed Dick Howser's champs by a margin of .269/.322/.412 to .252/.313/.401.

Starting pitching, however, favors the 1985 team with Saberhagen's Cy Young campaign (20-6, 2.87 ERA) and Charlie Leibrandt's 2.69 ERA. The bullpens of course were a different story. The 1985 team had AL saves leader Dan Quisenberry (2.37 ERA), but not much depth. The 2015 Royals had the more dominant closer with Wade Davis (0.94 ERA). And Kelvin Herrera (2.71 ERA), Ryan Madson (2.13 ERA), Franklin Morales (3.18 ERA), and a gutty Greg Holland (3.83 ERA) gave Yost an arsenal of late-inning weapons not available to Howser. Still, with the advantage in starters, the 1985 team held a team ERA edge of 3.49 to 3.73.

As for defense, the 2015 Royals led the majors in ultimate zone rating (50.9) and posted an AL best 56 defensive runs saved. These categories did not exist in 1985, but other stats indicate that the Royals team from that year was not as strong defensively. The 1985 team committed 127 errors to just 88 errors for the 2015 Royals. Though Frank White was still an outstanding fielder at second, Brett won the team's only Gold Glove in 1985. The 2015 team, in contrast, featured three Gold Glovers—Perez, Hosmer, and Escobar—along with three more first-rate fielders in Gordon, Cain, and Moustakas.

The 2015 team therefore holds advantages in offense, defense, and bullpen. Yost's boys, furthermore, won 95 regular season games and advanced through the postseason with an 11-5 mark. The 1985 team won 91 regular season games and walked an elimination tightrope through an 8-6 postseason.

The chess-inspired Elo ranking system further favors the 2015 club. That Royals team hit a maximum Elo rating of 1568.7. The 1985 squad lagged behind with a 1546.4 Elo mark. But the 1977 Royals and the 1980 Royals each achieved higher Elo ratings than either of the franchise's World Series winners. Should they be considered in this conversation?

Fueled by Brett's MVP season, the 1980 Royals were an offensive juggernaut (.286/.345/.413) that won 97 games and the American League pennant. The 1977 team, led by Whitey Herzog, relied on a powerful offense (.277/.340/.436) and strong pitching (3.52 ERA) to win a franchise-record 102 games. Except for defense and bullpen, the 1980 and 1977 squads look better on paper than the 2015 Royals. But there is one more factor to consider when comparing these teams: postseason results.

The 1977 Royals lost the ALCS in five games to the New York Yankees. Blowing a ninth-inning lead in the decisive playoff game that year still ranks as one of the worst heartbreaks in franchise history. The 1980 team similarly blew two leads in the eighth inning or later to drop the World Series in six games to the Phillies. Yost's team, in contrast, did not blow late postseason leads. They instead caused other teams to blow late leads with their unrelenting tenacity and never-say-die attitude. Batting .349 with runners in scoring position in the postseason further underscores the 2015 team's clutch mentality.

While the 1977 and 1980 Royals were great regular season teams, their inability to win a championship cannot be ignored in this discussion. Delivering in the postseason matters in Major League Baseball. Teams work, sweat, and bleed all season not to finish with the most regular season wins and nothing else, but to capture the World Series. The 2001 Seattle Mariners went 116-

46, setting the American League record for wins. But they are not remembered as one of the greatest teams of all-time because they lost in the playoffs. Yost's boys won the World Series in 2015. That is the ultimate goal for any big league baseball team. And no other Royals team matches that squad's combination of offense, defense, pitching, and postseason success.

George Brett was right: the 2015 Kansas City Royals are the best team in franchise history.

Chapter 14

Future of the Monarchy

And so "The Process" worked. When Kansas City hired Dayton Moore in the spring of 2006, the general manager warned his new employers that turning the franchise around would take time. He was right. The Royals finished that year with 100 losses. Six more losing seasons followed. Moore urged patience, asking fans to trust "The Process." As the losses piled up year after year, this term became mocked. Some critics urged David Glass to fire his GM. But the owner remained patient, allowing Moore to continue the pursuit of his vision. And finally, success. If 2014's AL pennant did not provide validation for The Process, the subsequent World Series title certainly did.

Moore became a hero in Kansas City. ESPN.com named him a top-five finalist for its 2015 MLB Person of the Year. Opposing GMs sought to emulate their once-ridiculed counterpart. Kansas City's transformation became a blueprint for how to win a championship.

How did Moore do it? For starters, he did not overspend. As a small-market team with limited local television revenue, Kansas City could not afford to engage in bidding wars for high-priced free agents. On the other hand, Kansas City could no longer remain at the bottom of the league in spending. Glass had to open his checkbook to some extent to help Moore build a winning team. The Royals' $113 million Opening Day payroll in 2015 set a franchise record, but still ranked as only the 17th highest out of 30 Major League Baseball clubs.

With more than half the other teams outspending Kansas City, Moore had to make his dollars count. Emphasizing the amateur draft, scouting, and the farm system, he stockpiled cost-efficient talent, rather than chasing expensive free agent fixes. It took time, but the Royals developed a minor league system brimming with prospects. Focusing on the bullpen instead of pursuing big-ticket starters, Moore assembled a dominant reliever corps. The GM also targeted athletic players who could put the ball in play, rather than expensive swing-for-the-fence sluggers. No Royal topped 22 home runs in either of their two recent pennant-winning seasons. But the team struck out fewer times than any other during that span. And Moore emphasized defense, tailoring his roster to thrive in Kansas City's expansive ballpark. His team led the American League in defensive runs saved in 2014-2015.

In 2003 Michael Lewis published *Moneyball*, describing how Oakland's GM Billy Beane used statistics and advanced analytics to find cost-efficient ways to build a winning ball club. Since the A's did not have a huge budget, they needed to invest in players with skills that were overlooked by traditional scouting methods. Oakland reached the playoffs five times between 2000 and 2006, and the book became a bestseller. *Moneyball* then became a hit movie in 2011, with Brad Pitt as Beane. Oakland reached the postseason three more times from 2012 to 2014, but in the Moneyball era the A's lost eight of nine playoff series. None of Beane's teams won a pennant. Moneyball worked in the regular season, but in the postseason, not so much.

During its October runs in 2014-2015, Kansas City gained a reputation as an anti-Moneyball team. Stealing bases, bunting, and forgoing walks (big no-nos to sabermetric devotees), Moore's team seemed to win with a brand new formula. Some even declared that the Royals' success meant that Moneyball was dead. Not true. Rather than rejecting the philosophy, Moore and J.J. Picollo embraced it. Kansas City followed Beane's plan to assemble a team of undervalued players; Moore just emphasized different categories. Moneyball, for example, calls for acquiring players with high on-base percentages, especially batters who walk a lot. The Royals contact-hitting lineup did not walk much, but hit for a high average, and thus a high OBP. Moore also recognized defense as a category underappreciated by other teams. When hired, he told Glass, "We want an above-average defender at every single position." Mining this market inefficiency gave the Royals a significant on-field advantage. The same is true with Moore's emphasis on relievers over high-priced starters.

And, contrary to popular opinion, the Royals did not reject analytics; they just did not embrace it at the expense of traditional methods of player evaluation. The team relied on both its scouts and its analytics team to make player decisions. Kansas City thus represented a combination approach tailored to the franchise's unique characteristics. "We believed that with our ballpark, and with the way the Kansas City Royals won in the past we needed to be this kind of a team," Moore said, "a team that catches the ball, a team that puts constant pressure on the opposition, a team that closes down in the late innings."

It worked, even in the postseason. Especially in the postseason.

THE OFF-SEASON: GORDON WATCH

For the first time since their arrival in Kansas City, Dayton Moore and his front office staff entered the off-season as world champions. But their goals for the winter months remained the same as every year. With several players doubtful to return, the Royals needed to fill roster holes for the next season.

Twelve months earlier, most of the players from the 2014 pennant winners were coming back. But there were a few key departures. Nearly every move Moore made to fill these spots for 2015 worked out. Edinson Volquez, Kendrys Morales, Chris Young, Ryan Madson, Kris Medlen, and Franklin Morales all delivered significant contributions. And the midseason trades that netted Johnny Cueto and Ben Zobrist further strengthened the team for a postseason run. Even Alex Rios, the weak link of Moore's signings, produced in the postseason with a .271 batting average and six RBIs.

With this impressive track record, Moore and his staff went to work for 2016. Kansas City would lose several key contributors from its championship squad. Free agent Cueto signed a $130 million deal with San Francisco. No surprise. Few expected the Royals to re-sign the dreadlocked one. But the team did hope to retain the services of Zobrist. The versatile star and his wife Julianna further kindled these hopes when they named their newborn daughter Blaise Royal. But alas, Zobrist signed a four-year, $56 million contract with the Cubs. Ryan Madson moved on to Oakland, and the Royals did not re-sign Jeremy Guthrie, Franklin Morales, or Alex Rios. Greg Holland, moreover, would likely miss the entire 2016 season.

But by far the biggest offseason question for Kansas City, and source of angst for Royals fans, was Alex Gordon. As expected, the left fielder rejected his $14 million player option for 2016 and became a free agent. He thus hit the open market, free to field offers from any and every team interested in his services. Moore declared he wanted to re-sign Gordon, who stated that he wanted to remain a Royal. But weeks passed with no signing. November turned to December and still no deal. Rumors swirled about the mountains of cash offered to Gordon from other clubs that the Royals could not match. Reports surfaced that the KC front office, committed to not overpaying for talent, had made a lowball offer that Alex had no choice but to reject. National media sources speculated that Kansas City had little chance of retaining Number 4. Even his teammates thought he was gone. Royals fans braced for the horrible news that their longtime hero would wear another uniform in 2016.

Throughout December, Gordon's agent Casey Close called each day to update him on the latest offers. Every time Alex would ask, "Did you hear anything from the Royals?" Day after day the answer was *no*. But after Christmas came a glimmer of hope. Moore phoned Gordon directly. They had a productive conversation in which the GM shared his future plans for the team. Soon after, negotiations heated up. Finally the day Royals fans had hoped for arrived. On January 6, 2016, Kansas City and Gordon agreed to a four-year $72 million deal. The longest tenured Royal would be back. The player who most personified the team's identity would return. The "hometown kid" who cut his teeth during the lean years and became the quiet leader of the revitalized Royals would remain in the family.

Kansas City fans rejoiced. Even beyond Royals Nation, the deal garnered praise. Despite the franchise-record contract amount, analytics experts endorsed the signing as a good WAR (wins above replacement) value. Traditionally-minded observers approved the deal for its impact on fan morale and team identity. "Alex Gordon wouldn't look right in another uniform," wrote Richard Justice of MLB.com. "He represents everything the Kansas City Royals have become and everything they can still be."

Moore made other moves. To solidify the bullpen he signed Joakim Soria, a coveted free agent reliever who closed for the Royals from 2007 to 2011. To restock the rotation, Moore inked starter Ian Kennedy to a five-year $70 million deal. Reflecting the rising expense of starting pitching, this was the second-largest contract in franchise history (behind Gordon's). Kennedy had stumbled through a lackluster (9-15, 4.28 ERA) 2015 season, but won 36 games for Arizona in 2011-2012. Though the size of his deal raised eyebrows, Kennedy was a high-strikeout, fly ball pitcher projected to improve in spacious Kauffman with first-rate outfield gloves behind him.

Doling out the two richest contracts in franchise history pushed the Royals projected 2016 Opening Day payroll to $130—easily a franchise record. Just a few years earlier, many

Royals fans blamed their team's mediocrity on David Glass's stinginess. Now the former Walmart CEO demonstrated his willingness to open the checkbook to put a contending team on the field. The man who hired Moore in 2006 to turn his franchise around proved that he really does want to win. And not just one title. Aware that many core Royals will become free agents after 2017, Glass knows the window for a budget-conscious team to compete for a title can close in a hurry. With the Gordon and Kennedy deals, he has put forth the funds to keep his team competitive while the core players are still wearing Royal blue.

ONWARD

With 2015 in the rear view mirror and the players reporting to Arizona and Florida for spring training, attention turned to the upcoming season. Writers, experts, and fans across the nation continued their annual tradition of preseason predictions. Would 2016 be the year for Chicago? Or Cleveland? Or Arizona?

For Kansas City, the question for the first time in 30 years was: Can this team repeat? Factoring in all the fancy statistics like wOBA, RC+, and WPA, advanced analytics provided an early answer. In February PECOTA predicted the 2016 Royals would win ... (cue drumroll) ... 76 games and finish *last* in the AL Central. Last? Really? Cue sound that Pac Man makes when caught by a ghost. In an equally dismal preseason forecast, FanGraphs ranked the Royals the 20th best team in baseball in projected WAR totals.

So according to the leading baseball analytics sites, Kansas City would return to also-ran status in 2016. There was something familiar about that prognosis. A year earlier advanced analytics predicted that Kansas City would flop in 2015. Remember the computer projections at the start of that season? The Royals did. And then they won the World Series. As Jeff Sullivan at FanGraphs wrote, "No team has more conspicuously made us look silly than the Royals."

To avoid further silliness in 2016, prognosticators might consider the following key factor: the core of Kansas City's championship squad will return. That means a lineup with Escobar, Moustakas, Cain, Hosmer, Morales, Perez, and Gordon. That means four Gold Glove winners, and two others who are Gold Glove-caliber. That means a rotation with postseason-experienced arms like Volquez, Ventura, and Young. And that means the top bullpen in baseball anchored by Herrera and Davis. Yes, there were subtractions, but Ian Kennedy and Joakim Soria represent promising additions.

Computer projections aside, with three straight winning seasons and back-to-back World Series appearances, Kansas City is a strong candidate to return to the postseason in 2016. But nothing is certain in baseball. Injuries and unforeseen circumstances always impact the course of a season. Following their 1985 championship, the Royals appeared poised to make another pennant run the following year. They boasted a formidable rotation with four excellent starters. Brett was coming off one of his best seasons at the plate. Dan Quisenberry had led the AL in saves four straight years. But injuries riddled the KC roster in 1986. A brain tumor forced beloved manager Dick Howser from the dugout. The defending-champion Royals finished with a losing record. And in a development no one at the time would have predicted, the team did not return to the postseason for nearly three decades.

Nobody, not even the powerful computers with their advanced analytic models, can predict all the events in a coming season. Too many variables. Too many moving parts. Too many competing teams. But the Royals have one consistent factor working in their favor: chemistry.

While other teams can and will outspend the Royals, they cannot buy the clubhouse camaraderie that has formed in Kansas City. Even players on other teams noticed the friendships among the Boys in Blue. "But the Royals ... have a deeper connection because that whole nucleus came up together and played together," observed Tigers third baseman Nick Castellanos.

"They went through all the ups and downs, and it shows in how well they play the game now."

The Royals not only developed a strong team character, but a team with lively characters who enjoyed each other and their jobs. This is evident in how they rallied together when one of their own was targeted on the field. It also showed in their frequent interactions with fans at the ballpark and on social media sites. In Ned Yost, moreover, they have a manager who allows his players to be themselves. He trusts them, despite their crazy handshakes and strange 1738 references. Summing up the Royals' characteristics, Kansas City mayor Sly James wrote: "Those guys are hardworking, friendly, classy, edgy, and fun. How could all of that rolled up in a single package not be charming?"

Not only charming, but inspiring as well. From the ashes of a crushing defeat, the Royals resolved to take care of unfinished business. Together at spring training in 2015 they set out on a mission. But they faced a daunting task. Baseball history is littered with teams that ended a season with heartbreak, hoping to reach the summit the next year. The 1986 Red Sox and the 2011 Rangers held multiple-run leads needing just one strike to win the World Series. The 1997 Indians took a one-run lead into the ninth inning of Game 7. The title within their grasp, all three teams lost. Did they return to finish business the following season? Boston missed the playoffs; Texas lost the Wild Card game; Cleveland lost in the ALCS. No matter how determined a team may be, it's not easy to climb all the way back to the top of the mountain.

But Yost's boys believed they could do it. Even though only once in team history had Kansas City won a World Series. Even though computers and experts alike said they had little chance to make the playoffs. They still believed. Other teams threw at them, looking to rattle the upstarts. The Royals answered these challenges. Significant injuries sidelined two starting outfielders, three starting pitchers, a second baseman, and a closer. The team weathered these storms and moved onward. Key players struggled. It happens. Keep working. Three Royals lost parents. Their teammates rallied around them. The team fell behind by four runs in the eighth inning of an elimination game. For most squads that would have been the end. Not this team. Not with their determination. Not with their heart. Like they had done all year, they kept the line moving. And it moved all the way to the World Series, where they faced not one but three formidable aces. The Royals fell behind in every game in the Series, but this time …

"The way it ended last year [in 2014], with everything that happened, such a magical run, you knew it couldn't end like that again," Eric Hosmer said. "You knew that story had to have a way better ending than losing Game 7."

Indeed it did.

Acknowledgments

Many thanks to Jodi Fuson for her estimable content review and proofreading skills. Like Wade Davis, she was an All-Star closer for this book. Thank you to Annie Pratt at USA TODAY Sports Images for helping me acquire many excellent photographs. Thanks also to Ron Kalkwarf for his fine photography work. I further appreciate the opportunities provided by Ron, as well as OLLI at UNL, to attend games at The K this past season. And much gratitude to Benjamin G. Rader for his instruction and guidance on baseball research and writing.

Finally, thank you to my wife Jill for her fervent enthusiasm for baseball and my writing projects. Her efforts and encouragement helped me to *keep the line moving* on this book.

Sources

Chapter 1

• Jerry Crasnick, "Royals' rally formula works again," ESPN.com, October 17, 2015, http://espn.go.com/mlb/playoffs2015/story/_/page/playoffs15_RallyRoyalsALCSGam e2/royals-comeback-formula-works-again-stunning-game-2-victory
• Jane Lee, "Gore steal overturned by Astros' challenge," MLB.com, October 12, 2015, http://m.mlb.com/news/article/154168742/astros-get-reversal-of-terrance-gores-steal
• Associated Press, "Royals rally on Carlos Correa's error to even ALDS vs. Astros at 2-2," ESPN.com, October 12, 2015, http://scores.espn.go.com/mlb/recap?gameId=351012118
• A.J. Cassavell, "The Royals' Defining Moment," Sports on Earth, November 3, 2015, http://www.sportsonearth.com/article/156300198/royals-world-series-champions-comeback-rally
• Bruce Schoenfeld, "How Ned Yost Made the Kansas City Royals Unstoppable," *The New York Times Magazine*, October 1, 2015, http://www.nytimes.com/2015/10/04/ magazine/how-ned-yost-made-the-kansas-city-royals-unstoppable.html
• Jerry Crasnick, "A Second Chance for Ned Yost?" ESPN.com, September 10, 2014, http://espn.go.com/mlb/story/_/id/11495935/kansas-city-royals-manager-ned-yost-lightning-rod-criticism
• Dave Heller, "1982 Brewers, Sept. 29: Yost's Big homer," *Milwaukee-Wisconsin Journal Sentinel*, Sep 29, 2012, http://www.jsonline.com/blogs/sports/171895861.html
• Doug Padilla, "Royals' cast of characters refuse to let season end," ESPN.com, October 13, 2015, http://scores.espn.go.com/blog/sweetspot/post/_/id/64316/royals-cast-of-characters-refuse-to-let-season-end

Chapter 2

• Vahe Gregorian, "Royals were devastated, then motivated, by 2014 World Series loss," *The Kansas City Star*, October 26, 2015, http://www.kansascity.com/sports/spt-columns-blogs/vahe-gregorian/article41499828.html
• Rany Jazayerli, "Pain Demands to be Felt," Grantland, October 31, 2014, http://grantland.com/features/2014-mlb-playoffs-kansas-city-royals-remarkable-run/
• Dayton Moore with Matt Fulks, *More Than a Season: Building a Championship Culture* (Chicago: Triumph Books, 2015), 5, 192.
• Vahe Gregorian, "No one can cast stones at Royals owner David Glass' house anymore," *The Kansas City Star*, Oct 24, 2015, http://www.kansascity.com/sports/spt-columns-blogs/vahe-gregorian/article41341293.html

• Sam Mellinger, "Series loss won't diminish Royals' magical season," *The Kansas City Star*, October 30, 2014, http://www.kansascity.com/sports/spt-columns-blogs/sam-mellinger/article3462717.html
• Tyler Kepner, "Still Hungry, the First-Place Royals Are Looking to Return to the World Series," *The New York Times*, May 14, 2015, http://www.nytimes.com/2015/05/15/sports/baseball/royals-are-still-thinking-about-the-world-series-this-years.html
• Pete Grathoff, "Data shows Royals' fandom spreading in all directions," *The Kansas City Star*, November 19, 2015, http://www.kansascity.com/sports/spt-columns-blogs/for-petes-sake/article45488946.html
• Tyler Kepner, "Now, Royals Can Do No Wrong," *The New York Times*, October 15, 2014, http://www.nytimes.com/2014/10/15/sports/baseball/now-royals-can-do-no-wrong.html
• Tyler Kepner, "Royals Envisioned Success, and Then Saw It Through," *The New York Times*, October 15, 2014, http://www.nytimes.com/2014/10/17/sports/baseball/the-royals-had-a-vision-and-saw-it-all-the-way-through.html
• Jason Gay, "The Kansas City Royals Want to Rule the World," *The Wall Street Journal*, October 20, 2014, http://www.wsj.com/articles/the-kansas-city-royals-want-to-rule-the-world-1413760648
• Jerry Crasnick, "Dayton Moore's vision validated," ESPN.com, September 30, 2014, http://espn.go.com/mlb/playoffs/2014/story/_/id/11617063/dayton-moore-vision-kansas-royals-validated
• Peggy Breit, "Fans show gratitude to Royals for thrilling postseason ride," KMBC.com, October 30, 2014, http://www.kmbc.com/news/fans-show-gratitude-to-royals-for-thrilling-postseason-ride/29437708
• James Dornbrook, "Royals win highest season attendance since 1991," *Kansas City Business Journal*, September 30, 2014, http://www.bizjournals.com/kansascity/news/2014/09/30/kansas-city-royals-2014-season-attendance.html
• Barry Svrluga, "The Royals can't escape 2014, which changed baseball in Kansas City," *The Washington Post*, October 17, 2015, https://www.washingtonpost.com/news/sports/wp/2015/10/27/the-royals-cant-escape-2014-which-changed-baseball-in-kansas-city/

Chapter 3
• Craig Brown, "Fact Checking David Glass," Royals Review, November 29, 2012, http://www.royalsreview.com/2012/11/29/3707028/fact-checking-david-glass
• Sam Mellinger, "Inside how the best Royals team in at least 30 years was built," *The Kansas City Star*, October 26, 2015, http://www.kansascity.com/sports/spt-columns-blogs/sam-mellinger/article41507676.html

• ESPN.com news services, "Source: James Shields to Padres," ESPN.com, February 28, 2015, http://espn.go.com/mlb/story/_/id/12299791/james-shields-reaches-deal-san-diego-padres

• Associated Press, "Edinson Volquez gets $20M over 2," ESPN.com, December 29, 2014, http://espn.go.com/mlb/story/_/id/12093863/kansas-city-royals-announce-edinson-volquez-signing

• ESPN.com news services, "Kendrys Morales joins Royals," ESPN.com, December 16, 2014, http://espn.go.com/mlb/story/_/id/12038765/kendrys-morales-finalizes-deal-kansas-city-royals

• Pete Grathoff, "Once upon a time, Royals fans blasted team for signing Kendrys Morales," *The Kansas City Star*, September 26, 2015, http://www.kansascity.com/sports/spt-columns-blogs/for-petes-sake/article36509313.html

• Mike Oz, "Royals sign Alex Rios, hoping to find one-year contract magic," Yahoo! Sports Big League Stew, December 16, 2014, http://sports.yahoo.com/blogs/mlb-big-league-stew/royals-sign-alex-rios--hoping-to-find-one-year-contract-magic-062259769.html

• Mike Axisa, "Royals sign Kris Medlen to two-year deal with eye on 2016, not 2015," CBS Sports, December 18, 2014, http://www.cbssports.com/mlb/eye-on-baseball/24899987/royals-sign-kris-medlen-to-two-year-deal-with-eye-on-2016-not-2015

• Andy McCullough, "Dayton Moore proud of Royals young core's rising salaries," *The Kansas City Star*, Feb 29, 2015, http://www.kansascity.com/sports/mlb/kansas-city-royals/article10701359.html

• Joe Posnanski, "2015 Kansas City Royals compensation," JoeBlogs, April 29, 2011, http://joeposnanski.com/the-lowest-payroll-in-baseball/

• Associated Press, "Royals reset mindset entering spring," ESPN.com, February 18, 2015, http://espn.go.com/mlb/story/_/id/12343408/kansas-city-royals-head-spring-training-high-expectations

• Matthew DeFranks, "Gordon remains optimistic about speedy return after so-so spring debut," FoxSports.com, March 21, 2015, http://www.foxsports.com/kansas-city/story/kansas-city-royals-alex-gordon-so-so-spring-debut-anticipates-return-lineup-opening-day-032115

• Joe Posnanski, "Letter From Camp Uneventful," NBC SportsWorld, March 13, 2015, http://sportsworld.nbcsports.com/royals-relaxed-spring-training/

• Zach Hodson, "The 2015 RoyalsBlue.com Spring Training Awards," Royals Blue, March 31, 2015, http://royalsblue.com/2015/03/the-2015-royalsblue-com-spring-training-awards/

• Max Rieper, "Royals finalize 25-man opening day roster," Royals Review, April 5, 2015, http://www.royalsreview.com/2015/4/5/8347067/royals-finalize-25-man-opening-day-roster

• Jay Jaffe, "Believe It or Not," *Sports Illustrated: Kansas City Royals 2015 World Series Commemorative Issue*, 2015, p. 8.
• Pete Grathoff, "A look at 149 preseason baseball picks finds no one thinks Royals will be in World Series this year," *The Kansas City Star*, April 6, 2015, http://www.kansascity.com/sports/spt-columns-blogs/for-petes-sake/article17484698.html
• Matthew LaMar, "On predictions, evaluations, and what we don't know," Royals Review, November 4, 2015, http://www.royalsreview.com/2015/11/4/9660674/on-predictions-evaluations-and-what-we-dont-know
• Sam Miller, "Here's How the Royals Blew Past Their 2015 Projections," Fox Sports, September 16, 2015, http://www.foxsports.com/mlb/just-a-bit-outside/story/kansas-city-royals-projections-pecota-lorenzo-cain-wade-davis-volquez-zobrist-morales-091515
• Max Rieper, "Bovada has Royals odds of winning the World Series at 25/1," Royals Review, January 19, 2015, http://www.royalsreview.com/2015/1/19/7853401/bovada-has-royals-odds-of-winning-the-world-series-at-25-1
• Ned Yost caption quote from the movie *Bull Durham*, but you already knew that.

Chapter 4

• Associated Press, "Ventura wins despite thumb cramp, Royals rout White Sox 10-1," ESPN.com, April 7, 2015, http://scores.espn.go.com/mlb/recap?gameId=350406107
• Andy McCullough, "Royals pound White Sox 10-1 on Opening Day," *The Kansas City Star*, April 6, 2015, http://www.kansascity.com/sports/mlb/kansas-city-royals/article17573024.html
• Associated Press, "Royals remain unbeaten with 12-3 romp over Twins," ESPN.com, April 13, 2015, http://scores.espn.go.com/mlb/recap?gameId=350413109
• Vahe Gregorian, "A Journey to the Launch Point of the Royals' rocket arm," *The Kansas City Star*, January 23, 2015, http://projects.kansascity.com/2015/becoming-yordano/#7955736
• Vahe Gregorian, "Royals must address Yordano Ventura's emotional misadventures," *The Kansas City Star*, April 24, 2015, http://www.kansascity.com/sports/spt-columns-blogs/vahe-gregorian/article19380393.html
• Associated Press, "Royals take 1st loss as Gibson, Twins win 3-1," ESPN.com, http://espn.go.com/mlb/recap?gameId=350415109
• Mike Ulmer, "Jays' Rios the real deal," Canoe.com, August 24, 2004, http://slam.canoe.com/Slam/Baseball/MLB/Toronto/2004/08/24/599941.html
• Blair Kerkhoff, "Alex Rios officially joins Royals on one-year deal worth $11 million guaranteed," *The Kansas City Star*, December 19, 2014, http://www.kansascity.com/sports/mlb/kansas-city-royals/article4684416.html

• Associated Press, "Royals beat Athletics 6-4 in rematch of AL wild-card game," ESPN.com, April 17, 2015, http://scores.espn.go.com/mlb/recap?gameId=350417107
• Associated Press, "Reddick's 3-run homer sends A's to 5-0 victory over Royals," ESPN.com, April 19, 2015, http://espn.go.com/mlb/recap?gameId=350418107
• Associated Press, "Royals overcome 5 ejections to beat Athletics," ESPN.com, April 19, 2015, http://espn.go.com/mlb/recap?gameId=350419107
• John Sorce, "Who Exactly is Paulo Orlando?" Baseball Essential, April 21, 2015, http://www.baseballessential.com/news/2015/04/21/exactly-paulo-orlando/
• Vinod Sreeharsha, "In tiny Brazilian restaurant, KC Royals' Paulo Orlando draws a crowd," *The Kansas City Star*, May 15, 2015, http://www.kansascity.com/sports/mlb/kansas-city-royals/article21118017.html
• Matthew DeFranks, "From Brazil to KC: Royals' Orlando captures a dream in big-league debut," Fox Sports, April 10, 2015, http://www.foxsports.com/kansas-city/story/from-brazil-to-kc-kansas-city-royals-paulo-orlando-captures-a-dream-in-big-league-debut-041015
• Max Rieper, "Looking back at Paulo Orlando's career," Royals Review, May 4, 2015, http://www.royalsreview.com/2015/5/4/8469241/looking-back-at-paulo-orlandos-minor-league-career
• Scott Merkin, "Tensions boil over in Royals-White Sox fracas," MLB.com, April 24, 2015, http://m.mlb.com/news/article/120176696/tensions-boil-over-in-royals-white-sox-fracas
• "Once America's sweethearts, Royals now look like MLB's biggest jerks," Fox Sports, April 24, 2015, http://www.foxsports.com/mlb/story/kansas-city-royals-brawl-again-white-sox-athletics-angels-yordano-ventura-brett-lawrie-042415
• Associated Press, "Avisail Garcia leads White Sox past Royals in suspended game," ESPN.com, April 26, 2015, http://espn.go.com/mlb/recap?gameId=350424104
• Wright Thompson, "Morales made his mark in Cuba," ESPN.com, October 11, 2009, http://espn.go.com/espn/hispanicheritage2009/columns/story?id=4545541
• Enrique Rojas, "Hitting on all cylinders, all shores," ESPN.com, September 22, 2009, http://espn.go.com/espn/hispanicheritage2009/news/story?id=4492683
• Vahe Gregorian, "Through turbulent waters, Kendrys Morales has landed safely," *The Kansas City Star*, April 20, 2015, http://www.kansascity.com/sports/spt-columns-blogs/vahe-gregorian/article19111938.html
• Associated Press, "Duffy throws gem, Hosmer homers, Royals beat Tigers 8-1," ESPN.com, May 1, 2015, http://scores.espn.go.com/mlb/recap?gameId=350430107

Chapter 5

• Associated Press, "Royals bring All-Star closer Greg Holland off disabled list," *USA Today*, May 6, 2015, http://www.usatoday.com/story/sports/mlb/2015/05/06/royals-bring-all-star-closer-greg-holland-off-disabled-list/70904684/

• Andy McCullough, "Alcides Escobar returns from D.L. as Mike Moustakas leaves for family emergency," *The Kansas City Star*, May 8, 2015, http://www.kansascity.com/sports/mlb/kansas-city-royals/article20544558.html

• Jeff Zillgitt, "Big Floridian bashes homers, weighs options," *USA Today*, April 10, 2008, http://usatoday30.usatoday.com/sports/preps/baseball/2008-04-09-Hosmer_N.htm

• Patrick Fazio, "Royals barber says Hosmer cut still popular," KSHB 41 Action News, April 6, 2015, http://www.kshb.com/sports/baseball/royals/royals-barber-says-hosmer-cut-still-popular

• Andy McCullough, "Kelvin Herrera returns to Royals bullpen after six-game suspension," *The Kansas City Star*, May 14, 2015, http://www.kansascity.com/sports/spt-columns-blogs/k-zone/article20977365.html

• Tyler Kepner, "Still Hungry, the First-Place Royals Are Looking to Return to the World Series," *The New York Times*, May 14, 2015, http://www.nytimes.com/2015/05/15/sports/baseball/royals-are-still-thinking-about-the-world-series-this-years.html

• Brett Tomlinson, "Q&A: Chris Young '02, on Princeton and the Major Leagues," *Princeton Alumni Weekly*, January 3, 2014, https://paw.princeton.edu/issues/2014/01/08/pages/0484/index.xml

• Brandon Karsten, "Seattle's Chris Young, the Comeback Kid-er, Man," Designated for Assignment, Apr 21, 2014, https://d4assignment.wordpress.com/2014/08/21/

• Randy Covitz, "Royals sign 6-10 righty Chris Young and expect him in pitching staff this season," *The Kansas City Star*, March 7, 2015, http://www.kansascity.com/sports/mlb/kansas-city-royals/article12931733.html

• Andy McCullough, "One email ended the pain and saved the career of Royals pitcher Chris Young," *The Kansas City Star*, April 30, 2015, http://www.kansascity.com/sports/mlb/kansas-city-royals/article19974903.html

• Blair Kerkhoff, "Royals closer Greg Holland feels good despite missing game with sore neck," *The Kansas City Star*, May 20, 2015, http://www.kansascity.com/sports/spt-columns-blogs/k-zone/article21528261.html

• Associated Press, "Morales homers twice, drives in 5 runs in Royals' victory," ESPN.com, May 23, 2015, http://scores.espn.go.com/mlb/recap?gameId=350522107

• Annie Heilbrunn, "10 questions with Edinson Volquez," *The San Diego Union-Tribune*," July 28, 2012, http://www.sandiegouniontribune.com/news/2012/jul/28/10-questions-edinson-volquez/

• Vahe Gregorian, "By any name, pitcher Edinson Volquez is a crucial cog for Royals," *The Kansas City Star*, March 8, 2015, http://www.kansascity.com/sports/spt-columns-blogs/vahe-gregorian/article13061549.html

• Andy McCullough, "Edinson Volquez dominates Yankees as Royals roll to 6-0 win," *The Kansas City Star*, May 17, 2015, http://www.kansascity.com/sports/mlb/kansas-city-royals/article21244734.html

• Mark Sheldon, "Volquez has Tommy John surgery," MLB.com, August 3, 2009, http://m.mlb.com/news/article/6220010/
• Max Rieper, "What increased attendance means for the Royals," Royals Review, May 18, 2015, http://www.royalsreview.com/2015/5/18/8618909/what-increased-attendance-means-for-the-royals
• James Dornbrook, "Royals win highest season attendance since 1991," *Kansas City Business Journal*, Sep 30, 2014, http://www.bizjournals.com/kansascity/news/2014/09/30/ kansas-city-royals-2014-season-attendance.html
• Associated Press, "Gardner, Yankees rough up Guthrie, Royals 14-1," ESPN.com, May 26, 2015, http://espn.go.com/mlb/recap?gameId=350525110
• Andy McCullough, "A late bloomer, Royals outfielder Lorenzo Cain making up for lost time," *The Kansas City Star*, May 23, 2014, http://www.kansascity.com/sports/mlb/kansas-city-royals/article402287/A-late-bloomer-Royals-outfielder-Lorenzo-Cain-making-up-for-lost-time.html
• Andy McCullough, "Before he became a playoff star, Lorenzo Cain had to learn how to run," *The Kansas City Star*, April 14, 2015, http://www.kansascity.com/sports/mlb/kansas-city-royals/article18509165.html
• Associated Press, "Ross hits winning single in 11th, Cubs beat Royals 2-1," ESPN.com, May 31, 2015, http://espn.go.com/mlb/recap?gameId=350531116

Chapter 6

• Dick Kaegel, "Mom's support has Perez on Royals' fast track," MLB.com, September 22, 2011, http://m.royals.mlb.com/news/article/25066304/
• Rustin Dodd, "Royals' Salvador Perez has made journey from young catcher in Venezuela to World Series MVP," *The Kansas City Star*, Nov 2, 2015, http://www.kansascity.com/sports/mlb/kansas-city-royals/article42186705.html
• Dick Kaegel, "Perez a blossoming star in Kansas City," MLB.com, March 6, 2014, http://m.mlb.com/news/article/68805428/salvador-perez-a-blossoming-star-in-kansas-city
• Sam Mellinger, "Salvador Perez is the engine that revs the Royals," *The Kansas City Star*, October 1, 2014, http://www.kansascity.com/sports/spt-columns-blogs/sam-mellinger/article2450080.html
• Tyler Kepner, "Lights, Catcher, Action!" *The New York Times*, October 21, 2014, http://www.nytimes.com/2014/10/22/sports/baseball/world-series-2014-kansas-city-royals-catcher-salvador-perez-perfume.html?_r=1
• Andy McCullough, "Jason Vargas heads to disabled list with elbow injury; Yordano Ventura deals with ulnar nerve irritation," *The Kansas City Star*, June 13, 2015, http://www.kansascity.com/sports/spt-columns-blogs/k-zone/article23983246.html
• Associated Press, "Ned Yost becomes Royals' winningest manager with 411th," ESPN.com, June 19, 2015, http://espn.go.com/mlb/recap?id=350618107

• Tyler Kepner, "How a Disgruntled Ace Gave the Royals a Full House," *The New York Times*, Oct 11, 2015, http://www.nytimes.com/2014/10/12/sports/baseball/how-a-disgruntled-ace-gave-the-royals-a-full-house-.html?_r=0
• Jeff Deters, "Alcides Escobar big part of Royals' rise to top of American League," *The Topeka Capital-Journal*, July 13, 2015, http://cjonline.com/sports/2015-07-13/alcides-escobar-big-part-royals-rise-top-american-league
• Associated Press, "Royals lock up Alcides Escobar," ESPN.com, March 15, 2012, http://espn.go.com/mlb/spring2012/story/_/id/7692624/kansas-city-royals-royals-sign-ss-alcides-escobar-four-year-extension
• Associated Press, "Rodriguez pitches well in Boston's 7-3 victory over Royals," ESPN.com, June 20, 2015, http://espn.go.com/mlb/recap?gameId=350619107
• Gene Guidi, "20-year-old Venezuelan prospect dealing with death threats," *Houston Chronicle*, February 20, 2002, http://www.chron.com/sports/astros/article/20-year-old-Venezuelan-prospect-dealing-with-2067284.php
• Andy McCullough, "Omar Infante battles through pain and emerges on offense for Royals," *The Kansas City Star*, October 23, 2014, http://www.kansascity.com/sports/mlb/kansas-city-royals/article3338199.html
• Assoc Press, "Kendrys Morales, Alex Gordon homer as Royals snap A's 5-game win streak," ESPN.com, Jun 27, 2015, http://espn.go.com/mlb/recap?gameId=350626111
• Jeffri Chadiha, "Royals ruling All-Star voting for multiple reasons, all legit," ESPN.com, June 17, 2015, http://espn.go.com/mlb/story/_/id/13093905/why-kansas-city-royals-dominating-mlb-all-star-game-voting
• Mike Oz, "Ballot-stuffing Royals fans could make the worst hitter in MLB an All-Star," Yahoo Sports, June 15, 2015, http://sports.yahoo.com/blogs/mlb-big-league-stew/ballot-stuffing-royals-fans-could-make-the-worst-hitter-in-baseball-an-all-star-starter-214052264.html
• Andy McCullough, "Omar Infante may get voted into All-Star Game, but Royals could still seek upgrade at second base," *The Kansas City Star*, June 15, 2015, http://www.kansascity.com/sports/mlb/kansas-city-royals/article24530206.html

Chapter 7
• Associated Press, "Royals lose Gordon to injury, rally past Rays 9-7," ESPN.com, July 9, 2015, http://espn.go.com/mlb/recap?gameId=350708107
• Chris Oberholtz, Amy Anderson, and Neal Jones, "Family, friends say goodbye to Noah Wilson," KCTV 5 News, July 6, 2015, http://www.kctv5.com/story/29481450/family-friends-to-say-goodbye-to-noah-wilson
• Shannon O'Brien and Jason M. Vaughn, "Royals pick up bandage crusade where young fan left off," Fox 4 News, July 3, 2015, http://fox4kc.com/2015/07/03/royals-pick-up-bandage-crusade-where-young-fan-left-off/
• Clark Grell, "Gordon a World Series champ: His former coach likes the sound of that," *Lincoln Journal Star*, November 2, 2015,

http://journalstar.com/sports/huskers/baseball/gordon-a-world-series-champ-his-former-coach-likes-the/article_55571c00-4729-5920-ade4-d32e4a144e05.html

• Dirk Chatelain, "A path to stardom out of left field," *Omaha World-Herald*, July 13, 2014, http://www.omaha.com/eedition/sunrise/articles/a-path-to-stardom-out-of-left-field/article_e8215267-36b0-5c2e-87c0-c71f8e3e5ddf.html

• Sam Mellinger, "Like George Brett before him, Alex Gordon is the face of the Royals organization," *The Kansas City Star*, Jul 11, 2015, http://www.kansascity.com/sports/spt-columns-blogs/sam-mellinger/article27027403.html

• Ben Reiter, "As Royals thrive, Alex Gordon emerges as dark-horse MVP candidate," *Sports Illustrated*, August 20, 2014, http://www.si.com/mlb/2014/08/20/alex-gordon-kansas-city-royals-mvp-candidate

• Max Rieper, "Mike Moustakas talks hitting, Ned Yost, and Alex Gordon," Royals Review, Dec 17, 2015, http://www.royalsreview.com/2015/12/17/10288106/mike-moustakas

• Jerry Crasnick, "Royals help AL come out on top in All-Star Game," ESPN.com, July 15, 2015, http://espn.go.com/mlb/story/_/id/13258738/kansas-city-royals-justify-large-all-star-game-presence

• Jeff Deters, "Alcides Escobar big part of Royals' rise to top of American League," *The Topeka Capital-Journal*, July 13, 2105, http://cjonline.com/sports/2015-07-13/alcides-escobar-big-part-royals-rise-top-american-league

• Susanna Kim, "MLB All-Star Game: Why So Many Kansas City Royals Players Were Voted In," ABC News, July 13, 2015, http://abcnews.go.com/Sports/mlb-star-game-kansas-city-royals-players-voted/story?id=32417768

• Vahe Gregorian, "Royals' Mike Moustakas was 'always an All-Star' to his mother," *The Kansas City Star*, September 22, 2015, http://www.kansascity.com/sports/spt-columns-blogs/vahe-gregorian/article36249930.html

• Ken Rosenthal, "Mike Moustakas reflects on mother's passing after career day at plate," Fox Sports, September 13, 2015, http://www.foxsports.com/mlb/story/mike-moustakas-reflects-on-mother-s-passing-after-career-day-at-plate-091315

• Dick Kaegel, "Big-hitting Moustakas is wise beyond years," MLB.com, March 1, 2011, http://m.mlb.com/news/article/16779370/

• Sam Mellinger, "Mike Moustakas isn't really in a slump, and he's made it through worse," *The Kansas City Star*, Oct. 22, 2015, http://www.kansascity.com/sports/spt-columns-blogs/sam-mellinger/article40913295.html

• Associated Press, "Moustakas' 3-run homer leads Royals past Pirates," ESPN.com, July 23, 2015, http://espn.go.com/mlb/recap?gameId=350722107

• Jeffrey Flanagan, "Royals excited to acquire Cueto from Reds," MLB.com, July 26, 2015, http://m.mlb.com/news/article/138817754/reds-trade-johnny-cueto-to-royals

• John Erardi, "Johnny Cueto: From 'short and skinny' to All-Star," *The Cincinnati Enquirer*, July 6, 2014, http://www.cincinnati.com/story/sports/columnists/john-erardi/2014/07/05/john-erardi-johnny-cueto/12252109/

• Andy McCullough, "Here's how Johnny Cueto became the ace pitcher the Royals desired, and acquired," *The Kansas City Star*, July 30, 2015, http://www.kansascity.com/sports/mlb/kansas-city-royals/article29589532.html

• Jeffrey Flanagan, "Royals make another splash with Zobrist deal," MLB.com, July 28, 2015, http://m.mlb.com/news/article/139237664/as-trade-ben-zobrist-to-royals

• David Auguste, "Royals players are being fined for not dropping Fetty Wap lyrics in interviews," ESPN.com, October 8, 2015, http://espn.go.com/espn/story/_/page/instantawesome-RoyalsFetty150729/

Chapter 8

• ESPN.com news services, "Edinson Volquez pelts Josh Donaldson in K.C. loss to set off fireworks," ESPN.com, Aug 3, 2015, http://espn.go.com/mlb/recap?gameId=350802114

• Andy McCullough, "Danny Duffy revamps physique in hopes of pitching 200 innings for Royals in 2015," *The Kansas City Star*, February 20, 2015, http://www.kansascity.com/sports/mlb/kansas-city-royals/article10771709.html

• Andy McCullough, "Danny Duffy may be struggling, but his desire to win runs deep," *The Kansas City Star*, May 2, 2015, http://www.kansascity.com/sports/mlb/kansas-city-royals/article348438/Danny-Duffy-may-be-struggling-but-his-desire-to-win-runs-deep.html

• Associated Press, "Morales, Perez each drive in 2, KC beats White Sox 7-6," ESPN.com, August 8, 2015, http://espn.go.com/mlb/recap?gameId=350808107

• Ken Rosenthal, "Mike Moustakas reflects on mother's passing after career day at plate," Fox Sports, September 13, 2015, http://www.foxsports.com/mlb/story/mike-moustakas-reflects-on-mother-s-passing-after-career-day-at-plate-091315

• Jesse Sanchez, "Herrera hopes to call home with Major news," MLB.com, March 14, 2012, http://m.mlb.com/news/article/27263892/

• "Top 100 Royals: #46 Kelvin Herrera," Royals Authority, June 2, 2014, http://www.royalsauthority.com/top-100-royals-98-kelvin-herrera-%E2%88%99-rhp-%E2%88%99-2011-present/

• Andy McCullough, "Royals reliever Kelvin Herrera stands tall on the mound," *The Kansas City Star*, July 11, 2015, http://www.kansascity.com/sports/mlb/kansas-city-royals/article27021094.html

• Jeffrey Flanagan, "Herrera, Davis thrilled for All-Star opportunity," MLB.com, July 7, 2015, http://m.mlb.com/news/article/135242208/kelvin-herrera-wade-davis-give-royals-6-stars

• Bob Nightengale, "Memory of late stepbrother fuels Royals' Davis," *USA Today*, August 6, 2015, http://www.usatoday.com/story/sports/mlb/royals/2015/08/06/wade-davis-kansas-city-kc-royals-brother/31267913/

• Marcus A. Grayson, "Wade Davis' mother recalls early years," WTSP 10 News, November 3, 2015, http://www.wtsp.com/story/news/local/2015/11/03/wade-davis-mother-recalls-early-years/75111886/
• Rob Rogacki, "Royals trade Wil Myers to Tampa Bay for James Shields and Wade Davis, but how does this impact the Tigers?" Bless You Boys, December 10, 2012, http://www.blessyouboys.com/2012/12/10/3749608/kansas-city-royals-trade-wil-myers-tampa-bay-james-shields-wade-davis
• Andy McCullough, "All-Star Wade Davis continually sharpens his mind and body," *The Kansas City Star*, July 10, 2015, http://www.kansascity.com/sports/mlb/kansas-city-royals/article26986183.html
• Matthew LaMar, "The Legend of Wade Davis," Royals Review, October 26, 2015, http://www.royalsreview.com/2015/10/26/9599654/the-legend-of-wade-davis
• Keith Jarrett, "An October to remember for Greg Holland," *Asheville Citizen-Times*, October 18, 2014, http://www.citizen-times.com/story/sports/2014/10/18/october-remember-greg-holland/17499337/
• John Perrotto, "The Best Closer You Don't Know," Sports On Earth, September 13, 2013, http://www.sportsonearth.com/article/60372520/
• Andy McCullough, "Royals closer Greg Holland to undergo Tommy John surgery Friday," *The Kansas City Star*, September 29, 2015, http://www.kansascity.com/sports/spt-columns-blogs/k-zone/article36988086.html
• Blair Kerkhoff, "Royals sign right-hander Kris Medlen to two-year contract worth $8.5 million guaranteed," *The Kansas City Star*, December 18, 2014, http://www.kansascity.com/sports/mlb/kansas-city-royals/article4627212.html
• Kevin Ruprecht, "Franklin Morales has been surprisingly good this year," Royals Review, September 9, 2015, http://www.royalsreview.com/2015/9/9/9286425/franklin-morales-has-been-surprisingly-good-this-year
• Vahe Gregorian, "Anatomy of a transformation: Luke Hochevar wins World Series for Royals," *The Kansas City Star*, Nov 7 2015, http://www.kansascity.com/sports/spt-columns-blogs/vahe-gregorian/article43620696.html
• Andy McCullough, "The conversation that led Ryan Madson back to baseball, and the Royals' bullpen," *The Kansas City Star*, October 7, 2015, http://www.kansascity.com/sports/mlb/kansas-city-royals/article38138277.html
• Associated Press, "Yordano Ventura overpowering as Royals beat Orioles," ESPN.com, Aug 27, 2015, http://scores.espn.go.com/mlb/recap?gameId=350827107

Chapter 9

• Max Rieper, "Alex Gordon activated; Royals make September callups," Royals Review, September 1, 2015, http://www.royalsreview.com/2015/9/1/9241525/alex-gordon-activated-royals-make-september-callups

• Blair Kerkhoff, "Franchise Four brings Frank White back to Kauffman Stadium," *The Kansas City Star*, Sept 1, 2015, http://www.kansascity.com/sports/mlb/kansas-city-royals/article33293640.html

• Associated Press, "Royals' Kelvin Herrera, Alex Rios diagnosed with chicken pox," ESPN.com, September 2, 2015, http://espn.go.com/mlb/story/_/id/13559868/kelvin-herrera-alex-rios-kansas-city-royals-diagnosed-chickenpox

• Max Rieper, "Royals set franchise attendance record," Royals Review, September 10, 2015, http://www.royalsreview.com/2015/9/10/9299853/royals-set-franchise-attendance-record

• Jeff Deters, "Royals' Jarrod Dyson stepping up with Alex Gordon out," *The Topeka Capital-Journal*, July 11, 2015, http://cjonline.com/sports/2015-07-11/royals-jarrod-dyson-stepping-alex-gordon-out

• Andy McCullough, "Jarrod Dyson is the Royals' engine who could," *The Kansas City Star*, October 18, 2014, http://www.kansascity.com/sports/mlb/kansas-city-royals/article3005416.html

• Hugh Kellenberger, "McComb's Dyson scores World Series-winning run," *The Clarion-Ledger*, November 2, 2015, http://www.clarionledger.com/story/sports/columnists/kellenberger/2015/11/02/mccombs-dyson-scores-world-series-winning-run/75030336/

• Associated Press, "Mike Moustakas drives in team-record 9 RBIs as Royals beat Orioles," ESPN.com, Sep 12, 2015, http://espn.go.com/mlb/recap?gameId=350912101

• Associated Press, "Royals shut down closer Greg Holland for season with elbow injury," ESPN.com, September 24, 2105, http://espn.go.com/mlb/story/_/id/13732776/

• "Jeremy Guthrie Profile," Stanford University, 2002, http://www.gostanford.com/ViewArticle.dbml?DB_OEM_ID=30600&ATCLID=208432354

• Max Rieper, "Looking back on Jeremy Guthrie's Royals career," Royals Review, September 24, 2015, http://www.royalsreview.com/2015/9/24/9378329/remembering-jeremy-guthrie

• Andy McCullough, "Jeremy Guthrie not surprised to be removed from Royals' rotation," *The Kansas City Star*, August 22, 2015, http://www.kansascity.com/sports/spt-columns-blogs/k-zone/article31923456.html

• Associated Press, "Royals romp past Mariners to claim first division title in 30 years," ESPN.com, Sept 25, 2015, http://espn.go.com/mlb/recap?gameId=350924107

• Marc Topkin, "Tampa Bay Rays' Ben Zobrist has taken a surprising path to today's All-Star Game," *Tampa Bay Times*, July 13, 2009, http://www.tampabay.com/sports/baseball/rays/tampa-bay-rays-ben-zobrist-has-taken-a-surprising-path-to-todays-all-star/1018198

• Vahe Gregorian, "Before he was a Royal, Ben Zobrist's baseball career hinged on a $50 tryout camp," *The Kansas City Star*, Oct 22, 2015, http://www.kansascity.com/sports/spt-columns-blogs/vahe-gregorian/article41120313.html

• Mark and Bruce Darnall, "Zobrist's Path to MLB included a Summer with AIA Baseball," Athletes in Action Baseball, 2009, http://www.aiabaseball.org/2011/11/zobrists-path-to-mlb-included-a-summer-with-aia-baseball/

• Jane Lee, "Zobrist to undergo left knee surgery," MLB.com, April 25, 2015, http://m.mlb.com/news/article/120445822/oakland-athletics-ben-zobrist-to-undergo-left-knee-surgery

• Associated Press, "Chris Young throws 5 no-hit innings, earns win one day after father's death," ESPN.com, September 27, 2015, http://scores.espn.go.com/mlb/recap?gameId=350927107

• Andy McCullough, "Royals starter Johnny Cueto rebounds after asking Sal Perez to change his setup behind the plate," *The Kansas City Star*, September 21, 2015, http://www.kansascity.com/sports/mlb/kansas-city-royals/article35958822.html

• Associated Press, "Cueto, Royals secure home-field with 6-1 win over Twins," ESPN.com, October 4, 2015, http://espn.go.com/mlb/recap?gameId=351004109

• Rustin Dodd, "#EskyMagic: No one can explain why the Royals are so good with shortstop leading off," *The Kansas City Star*, October 7, 2015, http://www.kansascity.com/sports/mlb/kansas-city-royals/article38121003.html

Chapter 10

• Andy McCullough, "Royals secure postseason home-field advantage with 6-1 win over Twins to end regular season," *The Kansas City Star*, October 4, 2015, http://www.kansascity.com/sports/mlb/kansas-city-royals/article37740321.html

• Brian Abel, "Kansas City Royals fans cheer on their team at the Take The Crown rally," KSHB 41 Action News, Oct. 6, 2015, http://www.kshb.com/sports/baseball/royals/kansas-city-royals-fans-cheer-on-their-team-at-the-take-the-crown-rally

• Jeremy Deckard, "Expectations elevated for Royals fans ahead of team's second straight postseason appearance," *The Topeka Capital-Journal*, October 8, 2015, http://cjonline.com/sports/2015-10-08/expectations-elevated-royals-fans-ahead-teams-second-straight-postseason

• Ben Lindbergh, "ALDS Preview," Grantland.com, Oct 8, 2015, http://grantland.com/the-triangle/2015-mlb-alds-preview-rangers-blue-jays-astros-royals/

• Barry Svrluga and Adam Kilgore, "ALDS Preview and Predictions," *The Washington Post*, October 7, 2015, https://www.washingtonpost.com/news/sports/wp/2015/10/07/alds-preview-and-predictions-keys-that-could-decide-rangers-blue-jays-astros-royals/

• Sam Mellinger, "Yordano Ventura controls his fire at right time for Royals," *The Kansas City Star*, October 3, 2015, http://www.kansascity.com/sports/spt-columns-blogs/sam-mellinger/article37613388.html

• Alyson Footer, "Zobrist's wife sings anthem at ALDS Game 1," MLB.com, October 8, 2015, http://m.mlb.com/news/article/153767310/ben-zobrists-wife-sings-national-anthem-game-1

• Associated Press, "Astros weather rain delay, Royals to win ALDS opener," ESPN.com, Oct 9, 2015, http://scores.espn.go.com/mlb/recap?gameId=351008107

• Associated Press, "Royals rally to beat Astros, even ALDS," ESPN.com, October 9, 2015, http://espn.go.com/mlb/recap?gameId=351009107

• Doug Padilla, "Royals cool, calm, collected like they've been there before," ESPN.com, Oct 10, 2015, http://espn.go.com/blog/sweetspot/post/_/id/63940/royals-cool-calm-collected-like-theyve-been-there-before

• ESPN.com news services, "Dallas Keuchel wins again at home; Astros take 2-1 lead in ALDS," ESPN.com, October 12, 2015, http://espn.go.com/mlb/recap?gameId=351011118

• Jane Lee, "McCullers can lead Astros to ALCS in Game 4," MLB.com, October 11, 2015, http://m.mlb.com/news/article/154055876/astros-lance-mccullers-ready-for-game-4-start

• AP, "Royals rally on Carlos Correa's error to even ALDS vs. Astros at 2-2," ESPN.com, Oct 12, 2015, http://scores.espn.go.com/mlb/recap?gameId=351012118

• Vahe Gregorian, "Royals, Chiefs and more: KC became the 'city that never quits' in 2015," *The Kansas City Star*, Dec 30, 2015, http://www.kansascity.com/sports/spt-columns-blogs/vahe-gregorian/article52352925.html

• Joe Posnanski, "The Walking Dead," NBC Sports, October 12, 2015, http://sportsworld.nbcsports.com/the-walking-dead/

• Doug Padilla, "Royals' cast of characters refuse to let season end," ESPN.com, Oct 13, 2015, http://espn.go.com/blog/sweetspot/post/_/id/64316/royals-cast-of-characters-refuse-to-let-season-end

• Vahe Gregorian, "Fueled by Moose's call, Royals' rally defies explanation but reflects relentless belief," *The Kansas City Star*, Oct 12, 2015, http://www.kansascity.com/sports/spt-columns-blogs/vahe-gregorian/article38885826.html

• Mark Twain, *Following the Equator* (Hartford, CT: The American Publishing Company, 1897).

• Jerry Crasnick, "Carlos Correa ready for anything, even an October setback," ESPN.com, Oct 12, 2015, http://espn.go.com/blog/sweetspot/post/_/id/64326/carlos-correa-ready-for-anything-even-an-october-setback

• Tim Penman, "Astros vs. Royals: Last-Minute News and Predictions for ALDS Game 5," Bleacher Report, Oct 14, 2015, http://bleacherreport.com/articles/2579207-astros-vs-royals-last-minute-news-and-predictions-for-alds-game-5

• Alyson Footer, "Royals salute fallen firefighters before Game 5," MLB.com, October 14, 2015, http://m.mlb.com/news/article/154487732/royals-honor-firefighters-in-pregame-ceremony

• Chris Oberholtz, Emily Rittman, and Laura McCallister, "Royals fans raise more than $100K for fallen Kansas City firefighters," KCTV 5 News, November 14, 2015

http://www.kctv5.com/story/30260932/royals-fans-raise-more-than-100k-for-fallen-kansas-city-firefighters
• Doug Padilla, "Johnny Cueto makes good on his Game 5 guarantee," ESPN.com, October 15, 2015, http://scores.espn.go.com/blog/sweetspot/post/_/id/64651/johnny-cueto-makes-good-on-his-game-5-guarantee
• Associated Press, "Johnny Cueto tosses gem as Royals oust Astros, reach ALCS," ESPN.com, Oct 15, 2015, http://scores.espn.go.com/mlb/recap?gameId=351014107
• Tyler Conway, "Royals advance to ALCS," Bleacher Report, October 14, 2015, http://bleacherreport.com/articles/2579326-royals-advance-to-alcs-highlights-and-twitter-reaction-to-celebration

Chapter 11

• Ben Lindbergh, "2015 ALCS Preview: Breaking Down Blue Jays vs. Royals," Grantland, October 16, 2015, http://grantland.com/the-triangle/2015-mlb-alcs-preview-toronto-blue-jays-kansas-city-royals/
• Mike Axisa, "ALCS Preview: 10 things to know about Blue Jays vs. Royals," CBS Sports, October 15, 2015, http://www.cbssports.com/mlb/eye-on-baseball/25340779/alcs-preview-10-things-to-know-about-blue-jays-vs-royals
• Mike Petriello, "How gravity-defying Estrada found the secret to success," MLB.com, September 22, 2015, http://m.mlb.com/news/article/150905866/marco-estrada-wins-with-movement-over-velocity
• ESPN.com news services, "Edinson Volquez wades through 6 scoreless innings as Royals win Game 1," ESPN.com, October 17, 2015, http://scores.espn.go.com/mlb/recap?gameId=351016107
• Jerry Crasnick, "Edinson Volquez comes up big for Royals," ESPN.com, Oct 17, 2015, http://espn.go.com/mlb/playoffs2015/story/_/page/playoffs15_VolquezALCSGame1/edinson-volquez-comes-big-kansas-city-royals-game-1-alcs
• AP, "Five-run rally against David Price sparks Royals to 2-0 advantage," ESPN.com, October 17, 2015, http://espn.go.com/mlb/recap?gameId=351017107
• Jerry Crasnick, "Royals' rally formula works again," ESPN.com, October 17, 2015, http://espn.go.com/mlb/playoffs2015/story/_/page/playoffs15_RallyRoyalsALCSGame2/royals-comeback-formula-works-again-stunning-game-2-victory
• Doug Padilla, "Royals' rallies keep putting leads in good hands," ESPN.com, October 17, 2015, http://espn.go.com/blog/sweetspot/post/_/id/64863/royals-rallies-keep-putting-leads-in-good-hands
• Jim Caple, "Game 2 collapse sends Blue Jays to Toronto in tough spot," ESPN.com, Oct. 18, 2015, http://espn.go.com/blog/sweetspot/post/_/id/64865/game-2-collapse-sends-blue-jays-to-toronto-in-tough-spot
• Associated Press, "Jays' bats sizzle at home; ALCS deficit to Royals shaved to 2-1," ESPN.com, October 20, 2015, http://espn.go.com/mlb/recap?gameId=351019114

• Anthony Castrovince, "A target for Bucs fans, Cueto shows rust on mound," MLB.com, October 2, 2013, http://m.mlb.com/news/article/62314146/
• Doug Padilla, "Road still filled with potholes for Royals' Johnny Cueto," ESPN.com, Oct. 20, 2015, http://scores.espn.go.com/blog/sweetspot/post/_/id/65057/road-still-filled-with-potholes-for-royals-johnny-cueto
• ESPN.com news services, "Royals hang 14 runs on Blue Jays to move within one win of World Series," ESPN.com, October, 21, 2015, http://espn.go.com/mlb/recap?gameId=351020114
• Jerry Crasnick, "Royals showing they are simply better than Blue Jays," ESPN.com, Oct 21, 2015, http://espn.go.com/mlb/playoffs2015/story/_/page/playoffs15_KCtakescontrolALCSGame4/royals-showing-simply-better-blue-jays
• Associated Press, "Blue Jays force Game 6 as Marco Estrada silences Royals," ESPN.com, Oct 21, 2015, http://espn.go.com/mlb/recap?gameId=351021114
• Jim Caple, "Marco Estrada pitches Blue Jays back to K.C., where spotlight shifts to David Price," ESPN.com, Oct 22, 2015, http://espn.go.com/blog/sweetspot/post/_/id/65267/marco-estrada-pitches-blue-jays-back-to-kansas-city-where-the-spotlight-shifts-to-david-price
• Doug Padilla, "Edinson Volquez steps up, then runs out of gas as Royals lose," ESPN.com, Oct 21, 2015, http://espn.go.com/blog/sweetspot/post/_/id/65271/edinson-volquez-steps-up-then-runs-out-of-gas
• Mike Axisa, "Confident Royals excited to head home following Game 5 loss," CBS Sports, October 21, 2015, http://www.cbssports.com/mlb/eye-on-baseball/25349032/confident-royals-excited-to-head-home-following-game-5-loss
• AP, "Royals repeat: KC beats Toronto, heads to second straight World Series," Fox Sports," October 23, 2015, http://www.foxsports.com/mlb/story/kansas-city-royals-beat-toronto-blue-jays-world-series-moustakas-zobrist-cain-hosmer-alcs-102315
• AP, "Royals edge Blue Jays to advance to second straight World Series," ESPN.com, Oct 24, 2015, http://scores.espn.go.com/mlb/recap?gameId=351023107
• Jerry Crasnick, "Royals march past Blue Jays for second straight AL crown," ESPN.com, Oct 24, 2015, http://espn.go.com/mlb/playoffs2015/story/_/page/playoffs15_KCadvancesALCSGame6/royals-mission-continues-world-series-return
• Doug Padilla, "Drama Kings: Determined Royals do it again," ESPN.com, October 24, 2015, http://espn.go.com/blog/sweetspot/post/_/id/65426/drama-kings-determined-royals-do-it-again

Chapter 12

• Jonah Birenbaum, "Yost: Royals 'expected' to be back in World Series this year," The Score, October 24, 2015, http://www.thescore.com/news/862223
• Mark Feinsand, "Royals ready to 'turn our power guys loose' on the Mets' young arms in World Series," *New York Daily News*, October 25, 2015,

http://www.nydailynews.com/sports/baseball/mets/royals-ready-turn-power-guys-loose-mets-article-1.2410189

• Mike Bauman, "Improved Royals team ready to take last step," MLB.com, October 26, 2015, http://m.mlb.com/news/article/155600504/royals-ready-for-next-step-win-world-series

• AJ Cassavell, "DYK: Top facts about Mets-Royals matchup," MLB.com, October 27, 2015, http://m.royals.mlb.com/news/article/155452870/top-facts-about-mets-royals-world-series

• Max Rieper, "Mets Series Preview: The World Series," Royals Review, October 27, 2015, http://www.royalsreview.com/2015/10/27/9614090/mets-series-preview-the-world-series

• Ben Lindbergh and Jonah Keri, "World Series Preview: Five Keys to Victory for the Royals and the Mets," Grantland, October 26, 2015, http://grantland.com/the-triangle/2015-mlb-playoffs-royals-mets-world-series-preview-predictions/

• Adam Paul Cooper, "Royals-Mets World Series Primer & Prediction," APC, October 27, 2015, http://apcblogs.com/2015/10/27/royals-mets-world-series-primer-prediction/

• Max Rieper, "Royals World Series odds, prop bets," Royals Review, October 27, 2015, http://www.royalsreview.com/2015/10/27/9621280/royals-world-series-odds-prop-bets

• Jon Heyman, "How much will Matt Harvey pitch? Innings limit debate coming to a head," CBS Sports, September 4, 2015, http://www.cbssports.com/mlb/writer/jon-heyman/25290191/how-much-will-matt-harvey-pitch-innings-limit-debate-coming-to-a-head

• Ted Berg, "Matt Harvey looks terrible in sudden drama over innings limits," USA Today, September 6, 2015, http://ftw.usatoday.com/2015/09/matt-harvey-new-york-mets-innings-limits-mlb-scott-boras

• "World Series national anthem performers and first pitch tossers," Newsday.com, November 1, 2015, http://www.newsday.com/sports/baseball/world-series-national-anthem-performers-and-first-pitch-tossers-1.11027361

• Associated Press, "Alex Gordon HR in 9th keeps Royals alive in 14-inning win over Mets," ESPN.com, Oct 28, 2015, http://espn.go.com/mlb/recap?gameId=351027107

• Enrique Rojas, "Source: Edinson Volquez learned of father's death before starting Game 1," ESPN.com, Oct 28, 2015, http://espn.go.com/mlb/story/_/id/13987854/2015-world-series-edinson-volquez-kansas-city-royals-right-hander-learns-father-death-shortly-game-1-start

• Jerry Crasnick, "United in losing their fathers, Royals duo help deliver Game 1 win," ESPN.com, October 28, 2015, http://espn.go.com/mlb/playoffs2015/story/_/page/playoffs15_VolquezYoungPitchPastLoss/united-losing-their-fathers-royals-duo-help-deliver-game-1-win

• Jayson Stark, "Royals finish what they started in epic Game 1," ESPN.com, Oct 28, 2015, http://espn.go.com/mlb/playoffs2015/story/_/page/playoffs15_StarkGame1/royals-finish-started-epic-game-1

• Associated Press, "Royals go up 2-0 on Mets in World Series behind Johnny Cueto's 2-hitter," ESPN.com, Oct 29, 2015, http://espn.go.com/mlb/recap?gameId=351028107

• Jayson Stark, "Royals look like an unstoppable October force," ESPN.com, Oct 29, 2015, http://espn.go.com/mlb/playoffs2015/story/_/page/playoffs15_StarkGame2/kansas-city-royals-look-unstoppable-october-force

• Jerry Crasnick, "Johnny Cueto spins a big win for Royals in Game 2," ESPN.com, October 29, 2015, http://espn.go.com/mlb/playoffs2015/story/_/page/playoffs15_Cueto/johnny-cueto-spins-big-win-royals-game-2

• AP, "Mets seize first win of World Series with offensive outburst in Game 3," ESPN.com, Oct 31, 2015, http://scores.espn.go.com/mlb/recap?gameId=351030121

• Jerry Crasnick, "Yordano Ventura's shabby outing leads to Royals' Game 3 loss," ESPN.com, Oct 31, 2015, http://espn.go.com/mlb/playoffs2015/story/_/page/playoffs15_VenturaStruggles/yordano-ventura-shabby-outing-leads-royals-game-3-loss

• AP, "Royals rally on Daniel Murphy's error, beat Mets for 3-1 Series lead," ESPN.com, Nov 1, 2015, http://scores.espn.go.com/mlb/recap?gameId=351031121

• Jayson Stark, "Murphy's error helps put Mets on the brink," ESPN.com, Nov 1, 2015, http://espn.go.com/mlb/story/_/page/playoffs15_StarkGame4/daniel-murphy-error-helps-put-mets-brink

• Jerry Crasnick, "Royals complete another comeback in Game 4 win," ESPN.com, Nov 1, 2015, http://espn.go.com/mlb/playoffs2015/story/_/page/playoffs15_/royals-complete-another-comeback-game-4-win

• David Schoenfield, "Game 5 pitching preview: Edinson Volquez versus Matt Harvey," ESPN.com, Nov 1, 2015, http://espn.go.com/blog/sweetspot/post/_/id/65857/game-5-pitching-preview-edinson-volquez-versus-matt-harvey

• Vahe Gregorian, "Showing pure heart, Edinson Volquez paves way to Royals' rally with own remarkable comeback," *The Kansas City Star*, November 2, 2015, http://www.kansascity.com/sports/spt-columns-blogs/vahe-gregorian/article42184143.html

• Jayson Stark, "Royals crowned kings of improbability and MLB," ESPN.com, Nov 2, 2015, http://espn.go.com/mlb/playoffs2015/story/_/page/playoffs15_StarkGame5/kansas-city-royals-crowned-kings-improbability-mlb

Chapter 13

• AP, "Royals outlast Mets in Game 5 to end 30-year World Series title drought," ESPN.com, Nov 2, 2015, http://scores.espn.go.com/mlb/recap?gameId=351101121

• Anthony DiComo and Jeffrey Flanagan, "Mighty KC! Royals rise in 9th, rule the World," MLB.com, November 2, 2015,
http://m.royals.mlb.com/news/article/156205900/royals-win-world-series
• Jayson Stark, "Royals crowned kings of improbability and MLB," ESPN.com, Nov 2, 2015, http://espn.go.com/mlb/playoffs2015/story/_/page/playoffs15_StarkGame5/kansas-city-royals-crowned-kings-improbability-mlb
• "Nov. 1 Ned Yost postgame interview," MLB.com, November 1, 2015,
http://m.mlb.com/news/article/156227886/ned-yost-world-series-game-5-interview
• Vahe Gregorian, "Showing pure heart, Edinson Volquez paves way to Royals' rally with own remarkable comeback," *The Kansas City Star*, November 2, 2015,
http://www.kansascity.com/sports/spt-columns-blogs/vahe-gregorian/article42184143.html
• James Montgomery, "Royals' Eric Hosmer on Partying Like a Champ, Pouring Beers on Paul Rudd," *Rolling Stone,* November 12, 2015,
http://www.rollingstone.com/sports/features/royals-eric-hosmer-on-partying-like-a-champ-pouring-beers-on-paul-rudd-20151112
• Lee Judge, "The Royals' World Series celebration was wild and long-lasting, and won't soon be forgotten," *The Kansas City Star*, November 2, 2015,
http://www.kansascity.com/sports/spt-columns-blogs/judging-the-royals/article42360141.html
• Sam Mellinger, "The biggest crowd you have ever seen came out to celebrate the Royals," *The Kansas City Star*, Nov 3, 2015, http://www.kansascity.com/sports/spt-columns-blogs/sam-mellinger/article42767697.html
• Associated Press, "Party time: Royals pack streets for World Series parade," Fox Sports, Nov 3, 2015, http://www.foxsports.com/mlb/story/kansas-city-royals-world-series-parade-champions-hosmer-perez-moustakas-escobar-zobrist-110315
• Mark Townsend, "Salvador Perez soaks Jimmy Fallon with ice bath on 'Tonight Show,'" Yahoo Sports," November 5, 2015, http://sports.yahoo.com/blogs/mlb-big-league-stew/salvador-perez-soaks-jimmy-fallon-with-ice-bath-on--tonight-show-044538891.html
• Jayson Stark, "Strange But True Postseason Feats of 2015," ESPN.com, December 30, 2015, http://espn.go.com/mlb/story/_/id/14439393/mlb-strange-true-postseason-feats-2015
• Jeff Sullivan, "Alex Gordon and the Royals' Defensive Dominance," FanGraphs, November 4, 2015, http://www.fangraphs.com/blogs/alex-gordon-and-the-royals-defensive-dominance/
• Adam Berry, "Alcides' 15-game hit streak most in 1 postseason," MLB.com, November 1, 2015, http://m.mlb.com/news/article/156232290/alcides-escobar-has-15-game-playoff-hit-streak

• David Laurila, "Sunday Notes: Series, Sveum, Pitching Coaches, Rays, more," FanGraphs, Nov 1, 2015, http://www.fangraphs.com/blogs/sunday-notes-series-sveum-pitching-coaches-rays-more/

• Vahe Gregorian, "Royals' AL Central title took root in Wild Card Game," *The Kansas City Star*, September 27, 2015, http://www.kansascity.com/sports/spt-columns-blogs/vahe-gregorian/article36752385.html

• Rob Arthur, "The Best Royals Team Ever Played Best When It Mattered Most," FiveThirtyEight, November 3, 2015, http://fivethirtyeight.com/datalab/kansas-city-royals-world-series/

• Darin Watson, "The 2015 Royals: Best Team in Franchise History?" Pine Tar Press, December 2, 2015, http://www.pinetarpress.com/the-2015-royals-best-team-in-franchise-history/

Chapter 14

• Jerry Crasnick, "The Case for Dayton Moore as 'Person of the Year' for 2015," ESPN.com, December 31, 2015, http://espn.go.com/mlb/story/_/id/14451932/dayton-moore-was-consideration-our-person-year-2015

• Patrick Saunders, "Kansas City's blueprint to winning World Series now envied, copied by MLB teams," *The Denver Post*, December 12, 2015, http://www.denverpost.com/rockies/ci_29242037/kansas-citys-blueprint-winning-world-series-now-envied

• Gershon Rabinowitz, "The Process of Building the Kansas City Royals," Baseball Essential, October 27, 2015, http://www.baseballessential.com/news/2015/10/27/the-process-of-building-the-kansas-city-royals/

• Peter Keating, "Welcome to the new Moneyball," ESPN.com, December 8, 2015, http://espn.go.com/mlb/story/_/id/14281753/kansas-city-royals-world-series-win-makes-new-face-moneyball

• Joe Posnanski, "Bucksense," NBC Sports, November 10, 2015, http://sportsworld.nbcsports.com/royals-play-small-moneyball/

• Sam Mellinger, "The longest winter: Inside the tense eight weeks when Alex Gordon was not a Royal," *The Kansas City Star*, March 12, 2016, http://www.kansascity.com/sports/spt-columns-blogs/sam-mellinger/article65700802.html

• Ashley Nickle, "Royals, Gordon land on mutually beneficial deal," *The Topeka Capital-Journal*, January 6, 2016, http://m.cjonline.com/sports/2016-01-06/royals-gordon-land-mutually-beneficial-deal

• Max Rieper, "Reactions to the Alex Gordon signing," Royals Review, January 7, 2016, http://www.royalsreview.com/2016/1/7/10723440/reactions-to-the-alex-gordon-signing

• Richard Justice, "Gordon is back where he belongs," MLB.com, January 6, 2016, http://m.royals.mlb.com/news/article/161169454/alex-gordon-royals-belong-together

• Josh Duggan, "Joakim Soria and the Royals agree to three-year deal," Royals Review, December 7, 2015, http://www.royalsreview.com/2015/12/7/9860252/royals-on-the-verge-of-signing-joakim-soria
• Sam Mellinger, "Ian Kennedy fits Royals' needs even if price was too high," *The Kansas City Star*, January 28, 2015, http://www.kansascity.com/sports/spt-columns-blogs/sam-mellinger/article57080813.html
• Max Rieper, "Royals fans finally like owner David Glass," Royals Review, January 14, 2016, http://www.royalsreview.com/2016/1/14/10765728/royals-fans-finally-like-owner-david-glass
• Max Rieper, "How Ian Kennedy's backloaded contract affects the Royals budget," Royals Review, Jan 27, 2016, http://www.royalsreview.com/2016/1/27/10840100/how-ian-kennedys-backloaded-contract-affects-the-royals-budget-2016
• Matthew LaMar, "PECOTA projects Royals to finish last in division with 76 wins," Royals Review, Feb 16, 2016, http://www.royalsreview.com/2016/2/16/11017880/pecota-projects-royals-to-finish-last-in-division-with-76-wins
• David Schoenfield, "The Royals, the Pirates and projections that go wrong," ESPN.com, January 25, 2016, http://espn.go.com/blog/sweetspot/post/_/id/67916/the-royals-the-pirates-and-projections-that-go-wrong
• Jon Paul Morosi, "Sorry, free-spending GMs, but you can't buy the chemistry the Royals have created," Fox Sports, January 22, 2016, http://www.foxsports.com/mlb/story/kansas-city-royals-hosmer-moustakas-gordon-cain-perez-escobar-world-series-champions-012216
• Lisa Gutierrez, "The 2015 Royals were sensations off the field, too," *The Kansas City Star*, November 4, 2015, http://www.kansascity.com/sports/mlb/kansas-city-royals/article42999867.html
• Joey Nowak, "KC Mayor James pens open letter to America," MLB.com, October 27, 2015, http://m.royals.mlb.com/news/article/155668036/sly-james-letter-about-royals-world-series

Among the sources consulted for this book, I am especially appreciative of Baseball-Reference.com and ESPN.com. The box scores, player stats, game-by-game schedules, play-by-play listings, and other baseball facts provided by these websites were once again vital to my research.

About the Author

Kent Krause writes content for online high school history courses and social studies textbooks. He holds bachelor's and master's degrees from Iowa State University and a doctorate from the University of Nebraska-Lincoln. In addition to his five books, he has published articles in *Great Plains Quarterly* and *The International Journal of the History of Sport*. USA Book News selected his novel *The All-American King* as a category finalist for the National Best Books 2009 Awards. Kent lives in Nebraska with his wife Jill.

Visit Kent online at: **kentkrause.com**